NEW HOPE, PENNSYLVANIA

River Town Passages

Compiled and written by Roy Ziegler
for the New Hope Historical Society

iUniverse, Inc.
New York   Bloomington

New Hope, Pennsylvania

River Town Passages

iUniverse books may be ordered through booksellers or by contacting:

iUniverse
1663 Liberty Drive
Bloomington, IN 47403
www.iuniverse.com
1-800-Authors (1-800-288-4677)

ISBN: 978-1-4401-0659-0 (pbk)
ISBN: 978-1-4401-0661-3 (cloth)
ISBN: 978-1-4401-0660-6 (ebk)

Library of Congress Control Number: 2008940900

Printed in the United States of America

iUniverse rev. date: 11/05/2008

Table of Contents

This book is dedicated to the founding directors of the New Hope Historical Society: Arthur J. Ricker, M.D., Eugene R. Lippman, Esq., Robert C. Bodine, Carleton Smith and Carl L. Lindsay, Jr., Esq.

This publication was made possible by a grant from the Pamela Minford Charitable Foundation.

Kaye Ballard, Pamela Minford and
Sandy Dennis at the Hacienda in New Hope

Pamela Minford – A Legacy

When Pamela Minford came to New Hope it was a country village that embraced the summer stock audience at the Bucks County Playhouse and the resident art colony. Drop into this quiet setting a dynamo, a visionary with business acumen exceeding her years and an uncanny sense of how to please her clientele. At 17, Pam opened her first business, an early American antiques shop in Manhattan, and then relocated it to Toms River, New Jersey.

Her best customer in Toms River was Ruth Page, owner of the antiques flea market on Mechanic Street. When Page retired in 1955, she convinced Pam to buy her property, the first of roughly two-dozen properties Pam would own in New Hope over the next three decades. With the antiques shop and its reproduction pine furniture workshop running smoothly, she renovated 5 houses on West Ferry Street into shops and opened The Peppermint Stick, New Hope's first ice cream parlor. Losing interest in pine, she rented her antiques shop and moved across Mechanic Street where she opened the Studio of Imported Interiors, filling it with furniture, chandeliers, and garden appointments from her travels to Mexico and Europe. Moving ever onward, she bought the property adjoining her original shop and built the El Patio Restaurant. With that, a restaurateur was born. Next she renovated 8 row houses on West Ferry Street that came to be called Regents Row. When her import shop patrons wanted more elegant dining she began building, atop the El Patio, what would become the 34-room Hacienda Inn, the luxurious country refuge for the likes of Maurice Chevalier, Liberace, Burt Reynolds and Dinah Shore.

As Pam's enterprises flourished New Hope flourished, growing into the tourist destination it is today. She brought energy, exuberance, style and flair to everything she touched. Pam touched New Hope, and was touched by it. Her commitment to New Hope remains alive today through the Pamela Minford Charitable Foundation, which has generously sponsored this publication on the 50th Anniversary of The New Hope Historical Society.

Nancy Wolfe Kennedy

Acknowledgments

Special thanks to Daniel Brooks, Deborah Minford Dailey, Reverend Joseph F. DiPaolo, Susan Eaton, Betty Ely, Carl Glassman, Sally Goodman, Journal Register, Nancy Wolfe Kennedy, Stephen T. Krencicki, Peggy Krist, Terry McNealy, David Newhart, Gordon H. Nieburg, Ann Niessen, Victor M. Rivera, Dee Rosenwald, Susan Sandor, Charles F. Tarr, Jane Till, Gene Underwood, Roger L. Whiteley, and Dennis Wise for the information and assistance that they provided in the production of this publication.

Cover design by Strenk Sandor Advertising

Introduction

Thousands of years ago a Lenni-Lenape Native American tribe carved its way east from the Delaware River through thick, richly wooded forests seeking land for planting, forests for hunting and water for fishing, settling on one thousand acres in what is now New Hope, Pennsylvania.

In the early part of the eighteenth century William Penn authorized the sale of one thousand acres of land to Robert Heath for the purpose of building grist or corn-support mill that would help to form a new community on one thousand acres of land then occupied by the Lenni-Lenape people. Penn had received the land as part of a payment for a debt owed to his father by King Charles II. The small tract was part of what is now the State of Pennsylvania.

The success of Heath's mill spawned the development of the first "village" in New Hope known as "Springdale" located on its westernmost boundary and, at its peak, included about two dozen homes and two very productive mills. The early families who settled in the town first known as Wells Ferry, then Canby's Ferry and, during the American Revolutionary War, as Coryell's Ferry before being named New Hope left a rich legacy of hard work, grit, determination and the Quaker tradition of hope for future generations. Indeed, New Hope became the industrial center of Bucks County, Pennsylvania by the beginning of the twentieth century.

During the Revolutionary War General George Washington marched through town on four documented occasions. His soldiers bivouacked there weeks before their famous crossing of the Delaware

River just a few miles south to wage the crucially important Battle of Trenton on Christmas night, 1776. Then, just two years later, General Washington led nearly ten thousand troops of his Continental Army from their winter headquarters at Valley Forge crossing in Coryell's Ferry (New Hope) on their way to the critically important Battle of Monmouth in New Jersey.

New Hope's strategic location on the Delaware River has made it an important transportation hub for the past three centuries. In the eighteenth century, horse-drawn stage coaches traveled the Old York Road, originally the trail which had been cleared by the Lenni-Lenape between the Delaware River in Philadelphia, on their way to New York City stopping at New Hope—the half-way point of the two-day journey. Later, barges floated down the glacier-created rock bottomed river delivering their cargo south to markets in the Philadelphia area. John Wells, the founder of New Hope, opened the first ferry operation that crossed the river to Lambertville, New Jersey around 1720. In the nineteenth century, when the construction of the Delaware Canal along sixty miles of the Delaware River was completed, New Hope became the central point through which three thousand canal boats traveled annually delivering coal, produce and manufactured goods to markets in Philadelphia and New York City.

The origination of the railroad in the late nineteenth and early twentieth centuries provided a more effective means of travel between New Hope and Philadelphia gradually replacing the canal boats. Then, in the 1960's, the Interstate Highway system revolutionized transportation making New Hope's one thousand acres easily accessible to millions of travelers within a radius of just a few hundred miles.

The great Pennsylvania Impressionist school of painters like Edward Redfield, Daniel Garber, William Lathrop and many others began arriving in New Hope and Bucks County in the early part of the twentieth century drawn there by the sheer natural beauty of the place first seen by the Lenni-Lenape people nearly ten thousand years before. When summer stock venues were created for Broadway play try-outs, New Hope's convenient location made it an ideal choice for their productions. Ironically, the Bucks County Playhouse whose stage was graced by such classic stars as Helen Hayes, George C. Scott, Robert

Redfield, Edward Everett Horton and many others was built into one of the oldest mills in New Hope.

The rather irreverent disregard for the preservation of historic structures and traditions that existed in the middle of the twentieth century led to the destruction of many historic buildings in the northeastern United States and threatened the existence of some of New Hope's historic legacies. Visionaries like Arthur J. Ricker, M.D., founder of the New Hope Historical Society in 1958, led local efforts to save the architectural treasures that identify the town's history today. His legacy has led to the preservation of more than one hundred buildings that are now included on the historic register owing in large part to the Herculean effort of Ann Niessen who completed the required research. The structures are located in a designated historic district tucked neatly along the Aquetong (Ingham) Creek, Delaware Canal and Delaware River within the one thousand acres that were once home to the Lenni-Lenape people.

Today, tens of thousands of visitors each week make New Hope one of the primary attractions for travelers in Pennsylvania. A growing number of analysts consider New Hope to be a top destination place for tourists and residents. The journey that began with the Lenni-Lenape people continued through the early families' pursuit of farming and industry. The drive for liberty and independence brought George Washington's army and the Underground Railroad there. In 2002, New Hope continued its spirit of acceptance of diversity. It became the first borough in the State of Pennsylvania to pass a comprehensive ordinance banning discrimination in employment, public housing and public accommodations on the basis of sexual orientation and gender identity. New Hope's location facilitated the creation of strategic transportation networks, and the beauty of the land attracted great artists. The town that gave new opportunities to young actors who became theater icons continues to cheer those who, today, seek stardom at its legendary theater.

New Hope, Pennsylvania is home to scores of art galleries, two museums, more than one hundred historic buildings and nationally acclaimed craft shops and restaurants. Live theater continues at the Bucks County Playhouse in Benjamin Parry's old mill. Local writers produce plays, movies and publications for new generations to enjoy.

In the center of it all stands the Parry Mansion, the eighteenth century home of Benjamin Parry, the father of New Hope's industry, preserved by the vision and dedication of Arthur J. Ricker, M.D., founder of the New Hope Historical Society in 1958 and his dedicated successors who have kept his vision of New Hope alive. This publication traces the journey of New Hope over the past three centuries as it has evolved from a farming and industrial capital into a popular tourist and residential destination.

Roy Ziegler

CHAPTER 1

The Native Americans

It is believed by some historians that the Lenni-Lenape Indians settled in the Bucks County area perhaps ten thousand years ago and may well have been the original inhabitants of the east coast of the United States. Indeed, their name is translated by some to mean "the original people."

Not long after settling here the Lenape began cutting the trail leading from the Delaware River in Philadelphia to the Delaware River in what is now known as New Hope as they migrated back and forth for their seasonal hunting, fishing and planting. That trail is still known by many today as the Lenni-Lenape Trail.

Nearly three hundred years ago, after the son of a Lenape chief revealed the trail to two blacksmiths in Philadelphia, men, first on horseback, then on carts, stage coaches, wagons and carriages began traveling the colonial route that had been built along part of the original trail. Leaving from the Old Barley Sheaf Tavern on Second and Race Streets in Philadelphia at dawn, the Swift Sure Stage Coach Company's coach and four set off up Broad Street on its journey to New York City. After a half a dozen or so stops along the way, the stage coach reached New Hope (Coryell's Ferry) by dusk. It was the half way point of the trip to New York City. Livery stables behind the old Logan Inn tended to the horses and carriages, and the hotel provided nourishment and rest for the weary travelers who still had a full day ahead of them before they would reach their destination.

When the routing of Old York Road's direction was changed from Reading's Landing in Center Bridge to Wells Ferry in what is now New Hope, it affected the development of New Hope for centuries to come. The old divergence of the Old York Road, now Route 202 and the Upper Old York Road, now Route 263 is clearly visible at the intersection of the two roads in Lahaska.

Remaining sections of the Old York Road weave through New Hope in fits and starts. A small part veers off West Bridge Street just east of Kitchen's Lane and heads across Sugan Road. It ends at West Bridge Street at the First Federal of Bucks County bank. Then just a few hundred yards east of the bank, the Old York Road reappears at the Free Library of New Hope and Solebury as West Ferry Street where it runs past the new Lenape Park at Stockton Avenue and on past the Parry Mansion across South Main Street to the Delaware River at the Ferry Landing Park. This is the site of General George Washington's crossing with nearly 10,000 troops during the Revolutionary War in June, 1778.

> **When the routing of Old York Road's direction was changed from Reading's Landing in Center Bridge to Wells Ferry in what is now New Hope, it affected the development of New Hope for centuries to come.**

Although times have changed over the past three centuries and it no longer takes all day to travel from Philadelphia to New Hope over the Old York Road, it surely can feel like an all-day trip, if one tries to negotiate the trip today. Journeying up North Broad Street to Rising Sun in Philadelphia, Jenkintown, Willow Grove, Hatboro, Warminster then on to Hartsville, Buckingham, Lahaska, Solebury and finally arriving in New Hope is a serious challenge to the patience of today's drivers.

The Logan Indian Sculpture

In September, 1990 the New Hope Historical Society arranged with Stephen Kates of the Logan Inn to bring back to the community a venerable old New Hope artifact known as the Logan Indian. The deteriorating remains of the metal figure were discovered in an outbuilding of the inn under a pile of debris. In the months that followed, the figure was completely restored and painted. A suitable metal pole was installed with the Logan Indian at the top on the Ferry Street side of the Parry Mansion lawn for all to see. Officially, the Indian was on "permanent loan" to the Society for the purpose of public display with all restoration, installation and maintenance costs defrayed by the Society.

The late Francis Curley was a native of New Hope and a long time Borough councilman and an active historian. He was treasurer and a long-time member of the New Hope Historical Society. The Historical Society has created the Francis Curley Scholarship that is awarded to a graduating senior of the New Hope-Solebury High School who has demonstrated community involvement and has committed to pursue higher education in history or the social sciences.

Curley related the story that Charles Buckman Knowles wrote in his diary for November 24, 1874: "The weather today has been clear, cool and a little blustering. Last night it was alarmingly tempestuous.

The papers this morning report great damage to property in various places. The big Indian that has stood on top of a high pole in front of (now Van Hart's Tavern) there six or seven years past had to succumb to the gale. He is so bowed and bent as to be quite unfit for duty. The pole where he stands is 65 feet in height. As far back as 1828 it was first erected. The figure of an American Indian with bow and arrow was drawn and painted by Samuel Moon, a young man from New Hope since deceased."

Knowles was in position to know. As Benjamin Parry's only son-in-law he made frequent visits to New Hope. On June 1, 1876 by motion of New Hope Borough Council, Andrew Jackson Solomon was instructed to remove the Indian Pole as it was in a dangerous condition and likely to fall and damage property and lives. Solomon, for his trouble, was to keep the pole and also be responsible for the damages," wrote Knowles. The next effort to display the Indian by the Citizens Literary Society in 1909 failed.

As far as it is known, the Indian remained stored in the Logan Inn barn until the summer of 1939 when Everett Miller repainted it and stood it on the grounds of the Logan. In the 1960's, when Carl Lutz and Art Sanders became owners of the Logan Inn, they placed the Indian on a pole. It was removed in the 1970's and stored at the Logan because the iron work needed repairs.

How did it all begin? Some confusion persists. What is clearer is that the Indian was constructed by Samuel Cooper at the suggestion of the inn's owner, Abraham D. Myers and that it was paid for by subscription. What is not clear is why it was put up. 1828 was the 50th anniversary of George Washington's crossing the Delaware in June, 1778 at Coryell's Ferry. Or was the Indian to commemorate George Washington's birthday or the election of Andrew Jackson? There is another possibility. The Inn would have been 100 years old at the time, and since the idea for the Indian came from the Inn's owner, it is logical to assume that may have been another reason. There is general agreement that the inn began to call itself the Logan starting around that date.

Why the Logan Indian? It was the custom for some Indians to take the name of James Logan, William Penn's Secretary, who dealt far more with the Indians of the Delaware Valley than Penn. We know of two prominent Chiefs, one in Germantown and the other from the Ohio Valley who definitely took Logan's name. The other possibility is the creek we know as the Ingham or Aquetong was once called Logan Creek after James Logan who owned the land....

It is most fitting that the Logan Indian still stands tall today to survey the community that the Lenni-Lenape first inhabited nearly ten thousand years ago. It also gives testimony to New Hope's appreciation for its rich history and for its continued focus on the importance of the arts.

CHAPTER 2

The Quakers

William Penn agreed to sell the land that is now New Hope to Robert Heath on the condition that Heath would build and keep in repair a water corn mill for the use of the neighborhood. And Robert Heath built the mill as promised between 1701 and 1702. It was the first of many mills to come over the next two hundred and fifty years.

And thus, New Hope was born. It was one thousand acres in one of the most beautiful, bucolic settings in Bucks County centered in an area still referred to as "Springdale" and part of the complex known locally as "the ruins" situated along the Great Aquetong or Ingham Spring along South Sugan and Stoney Hill Roads and West Mechanic Street. The land had originally been conveyed by William Penn to Heath's brother-in-law, Thomas Woolrich. But his queasiness about the prospect of traveling across a dangerous ocean led Woolrich to sell the land that he would never see to Heath.

Unfortunately, Robert Heath died before he could receive the patent for the land from William Penn. His son, Richard Heath, obtained the patent from Penn, but died very shortly afterward. The land was conveyed to his sisters and their husbands and was eventually divided up and sold.

The original section of the Heath House—1707

Thence-forth the numbers of owners of Springdale continued to multiply and change until the present day. Yardley, Holcombe, Brockden, Morris, Atkinson, Magill, Ely—many of the great, historic families of Bucks County took possession at one time or another over the past three centuries. Among the most prominent; Andrew Ellicott, one of the designers of the layout of Washington, D.C.; William Maris, who actually named the site "Springdale" and built the first major addition to the house; and William Huffnagle, who was the principal engineer for the construction of the canal and railroad through New Hope. He sold the "Springdale" mansion, often called the "Huffnagle mansion" to his brother, Charles, a physician, who became the first United States Consul to Calcutta. He was admired for his treatment of cholera among British troops there. When he returned from India just a few years later, Charles, in ill health, retired to "Springdale" and hired the great Philadelphia architect, Samuel Sloan to enlarge the house. Sloan was the architect of numerous well-known buildings in the northeast ranging from the Eastwick Villa near Bartram's Gardens to the expansion of the New Jersey State House and the design of the Eastern State Penitentiary. He also provided meaningful input into the design for the expansion of Fairmount Park in Philadelphia.

Charles Huffnagle delighted the New Hope public by opening Springdale every Tuesday to visitors. He had assembled a quasi zoo on the estate. It is reported that humped cattle from India, an Arabian horse, sheep, Syrian goats, pigs from China, ponies and an odd assortment of dogs had been housed on the grounds for all the public to enjoy. Huffnagle died in London in 1860 and various members of the family lived in Springdale until 1878.

The house was vacant for nearly fifty years until it was purchased by artist and engraver, Albert Rosenthal, whose changes to the building did it no favors. In the 1980's Edward Gerace's ambition to restore the integrity of "Springdale" fell short and he sold it without accomplishing his goal.

Although as architect, historian Margaret Bye Richie has noted, Sloan's expansion of the house destroyed one of New Hope's oldest and venerable houses most probably connected with the Robert Heath's first mill; part of Heath's original home still exists on the east side of the mansion.

Historic marker located at the site of the Heath Mill

Today the gorgeous Springdale mansion stands proudly as a beautiful and lasting tribute to Robert Heath who began the mill industry three hundred years ago and established what has evolved into New Hope. The many hundreds of people who navigate Sugan Road in their modern vehicles each day between the ruins of the Heath and Maris mills continue to give new life to the place where it all began. The New Hope Historical Society installed a historic site marker on the property to memorialize its great significance in the creation of the New Hope community.

John Wells settled in the area around 1715 and purchased about one hundred acres of the Heath property that was located along the Delaware River. Later, he obtained the first license to operate a ferry on the Delaware River at New Hope. He also received the first license to run an inn. He is considered to be the founder of New Hope. The town was named Wells Ferry until his death in 1748.

CHAPTER 3

Early Industry

The Heath Mill

Once a five-story fieldstone structure (one story below grade) whose construction and operation provided relief for countless farmers from miles around, the Heath mill now lies in ruins below South Sugan and Stoney Hill Road. This is a small slice of William Penn's vast land holding that was given by King Charles II in payment of a debt owed to his late father. It was sold to Thomas Woolrich whose fear of sailing to the New World led him to decline the option and sell it to Robert Heath. Heath's promise to William Penn to build a corn mill there was honored by him and his son, Richard around 1702. The mill became the first in a long line of mills that followed over then next two centuries. When Richard Heath died in 1712 the land was bequeathed to his five siblings who gradually sold off parcels of the original 1,000 acres.

But who operated Heath's mill? Margaret Bye Richie reminds us that historians have never discovered who actually ran the operations. It appears that Robert and Richard lived in the Bristol Township, Pennsylvania and leased the operations to a millwright whose identity remains unknown.

The New Hope Mills

Benjamin Parry is widely considered to be the "father" of New Hope because his entrepreneurship put the town on the industrial map of Bucks County. Parry arrived in New Hope, then named Coryell's Ferry, in the early 1780's to manage the grist mill owned by Dr. Joseph Todd, a friend of Parry's family. When Todd died, Parry purchased the mill and gradually expanded the operations to include a lumber mill, saw mill and flax mill. After rebuilding his fire ravaged mills in the center of Coryell's Ferry in 1790 and naming them "New Hope Mills" he unwittingly gave the town its new name.

The New Hope Flour Mills in late 19th Century

Parry boasted that he could produce three hundred barrels of flour each week and cut one thousand board feet of lumber a day. Parry was also a partner in Parry and Cresson, a flour commission and storage business in Philadelphia. He invented a process for preserving corn and grain for overseas shipping that considerably opened the markets to trade. By the end of the 1790's Benjamin Parry owned more than sixteen acres in what is now the center of New Hope. Parry was known for his extensive involvement and interest in the continual improvement of his community.

> After rebuilding his fire-ravaged mills in the center of Coryell's Ferry in 1790 and naming them "New Hope Mills" he (Benjamin Parry) unwittingly gave the town its new name (New Hope). It was officially incorporated in 1837.

Benjamin Parry, with the help of his influential partners including Samuel Ingham, a three-term congressman and Treasurer of the United States under the Andrew Jackson administration, led the drive to build the first bridge to Lambertville, New Jersey; opened the first bank in New Hope and financed the construction of the Delaware Canal through the borough. His nephew, John C. Parry, was a founding member of the New Hope Eagle Fire Company and was elected the first burgess or mayor of New Hope when it was incorporated in 1837. Benjamin Parry died at the age of eighty-two years in 1839 in the Parry Mansion.

The Maris Mills

William Maris built the mill, part of which still stands on the east side of Sugan Road in 1813 shortly after his arrival in New Hope from Philadelphia. He bought up the old Heath mill and property and enlarged the home known as Springdale. Maris was a major player in the New Hope industry at this time and a chief rival of Benjamin Parry. Their bitter lawsuit over use of the Aquetong Creek lasted about ten years with Maris coming out on the losing end of the deal. After a fire partially destroyed his mill in 1836, Maris rebuilt the mill, but left town under a cloud of bankruptcy which was not all that uncommon at the time. Maris's mill and part of the property was eventually purchased by Joshua Whiteley in 1864. It has undergone some drastic revisions and reconstruction over the past thirty years or so, and has been used as a residence, bed and breakfast and for commercial purposes. The old Maris mill now vacant and falling into disrepair seems to need another suitor to bring about yet another reconstruction nearly two hundred years after Maris made his presence known in town by building the tall, formidable structure.

**William Maris's silk mill on the left,
On the right is the old Heath Mill**

Shortly after arriving in New Hope from Philadelphia in 1812 William Maris began construction of some of the town's most celebrated buildings. First, acquiring the original Heath Mill on Sugan Road, Maris then built the huge cotton mill whose shell now houses a sprawling residence. Next, he enlarged the original Heath home naming it "Springdale," an area much revered today. He completed construction of the Delaware House Hotel which, nearly two hundred years later, remains one of New Hope's landmarks at the gateway from New Jersey. Later, he again dazzled the town with the completion of the twin mills located on what is now Old Mill Road. Today, the larger remaining tower provides spacious housing in a forest-like setting.

> **(Maris's) Lepanto Mills significantly contributed to New Hope's becoming the veritable industrial capital of Bucks County at the time.**

William Maris's rivalry with Benjamin Parry peaked at around the time that Maris built his flax mills, the Lepanto Mills, on what is now known as The Old Mill Apartments around 1825. These were "twin mills" that demonstrated Maris's prestige to a New Hope community that must have been entertained by the one-upmanship of the Maris and Parry contest for community dominance. Imagine the stories that must have been traded at the old Logan Inn and Delaware House Hotel when locals gathered to recount the latest projects planned by those local entrepreneurs. And, yes, not unlike today, those two local tycoons were battling in court about the use of the Aquetong Creek that powered their respective mills. Benjamin Parry, who had obtained control of the creek through his friend and partner, Congressman Samuel Ingham, eventually won the court case after ten bitter years of litigation.

The Lepanto Mills significantly contributed to New Hope's becoming the veritable industrial capital of Bucks County at the time. They produced flax and rope for at least thirty-five years and once were owned by William Umpleby, whose home is now a fashionable Bed and Breakfast Inn on West Bridge Street, just about one block from the mills. The west side of the twin mills that stood about two and a half stories high, slid into ruins many decades ago.

A four and a half story structure remains on the east side of what had been the twin mills. It was converted into apartments around 1976, providing spacious residences in a spectacular, wooded setting along the north bank of the fabled Ingham (Aquetong) Creek. This is a fieldstone structure in the Bucks Country tradition. Its slate roof and numerous six over six pane windows, now trimmed in bright white paint, give this old mill a touch of elegance that is unexpected when turning off West Ferry Street on to the old road that once led to some of the largest mills in Bucks County. Many of the homes in this neighborhood once housed the hundreds of townsfolk who, employed at the mills, benefited greatly from the rivalry of William Maris and Benjamin Parry for community and economic dominance.

Union Mills

The great Bucks County historian, W.W.H. Davis said that in his day and generation New Hope "…had no more useful and enterprising citizen than the late Lewis S. Coryell," and that…he was one of the best practical engineers in the state." There is probably no greater testimony to the truth of this statement than the marvelous Union Mills complex on South Main Street in New Hope.

> **In his day and generation New Hope had no more useful and enterprising citizen than...Lewis S. Coryell...and he was one of the best practical engineers in the state.**

Construction of this maze of stone and brick structures was probably begun by Lewis S. Coryell, an engineer and builder, and William Maris, a designer around 1820. As a water/steam-powered paper mill it provided a livelihood to generations of New Hope workers for nearly one and a half centuries until closing in the early 1970's.

Union Mills was built on a site that was once called Malta Island. During the Revolutionary War George Washington's troops hid many of the Durham boats on the island that were used in General Washington's surprise attack on the Hessians in Trenton in 1776 that turned the course of the war.

Water pumped from the Delaware River powered the mill

Coryell's genius is evident in the design and construction of a water wheel at the mill that pumped water into the canal from the Delaware River that was in use for more than a hundred years until it was washed away in the flood of 1936. Coryell was involved in the construction of the canal and most probably bought the parcel of land to augment his position when the canal was built. He also designed and built the Wells Wing dam at the site across to Lambertville.

Benjamin Parry had built a mill across the wing dam just outside of Lambertville.

Union Mills in the early 1900's

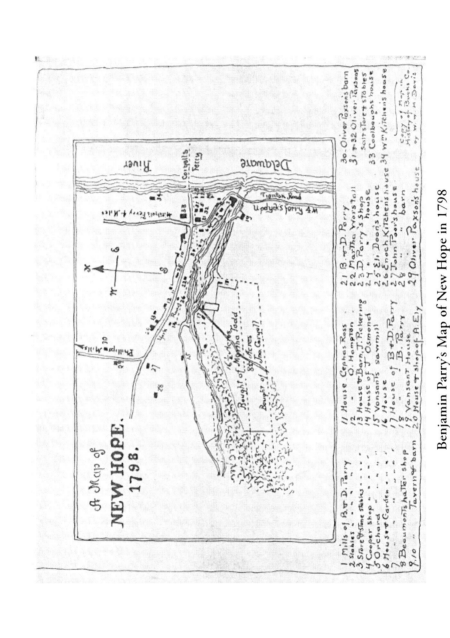

Benjamin Parry's Map of New Hope in 1798

CHAPTER 4

Early Families and Homes

The Joshua Van Sant House—1743

There is an interesting and rather ironic relationship between the Van Sant House located at 4 West Mechanic Street and the Coryell House, now the Havana nightclub, just around the corner at 105 South Main Street.

Ichabod Wilkinson moved from Rhode Island to Bucks County around 1742. He purchased land once owned by New Hope's founder, John Wells, and built the home now known as the Van Sant House in 1743. Wilkinson was an ironmaster who built a rolling and slitting mill which produced nails for the growing Bucks County community. His mill was located in the area that is now the north end of the aqueduct on the Delaware Canal over the Aquetong Creek.

The Van Sant house is, most probably, the oldest house in New Hope. Part of the house located across the street at 6 East Mechanic Street is said to have been built by Wilkinson around 1740, and part of the Paxson-Rhoads estate on West Bridge Street may have been built before 1740.

The Joshua Van Sant House Today

This charming, fieldstone home partially covered with stucco is named for Joshua Van Sant, the husband of Ichabod Wilkinson's daughter, Mary. It is a dream house with a fire place in every room. Van Sant was a much respected builder whom records show was hired by Benjamin Parry to work on his mill.

The Coryell House located just down South Main Street from the Van Sant House was once the home of Lewis S. Coryell who married Van Sant's daughter, Mary. It appears that Mary's father, Joshua, was unhappy with her choice for a husband. Records indicate that, although he gave his land to his daughter; he insisted that Lewis S. Coryell, her husband, was never to acquire the property. Alas, as it often happens in family differences, Mary Van Sant bequeathed the house to Lewis when she died in 1834, contrary to the wishes of her father.

During renovations to the Van Sant House in the late nineteenth century, grapeshot believed to have been fired by the British in 1776 from Goat Hill across the Delaware River in Lambertville, New Jersey was found imbedded in the roof.

The Paxson-Rhoads Estate—c. 1760

When ten generations of a family continue to occupy land that was the largest tract of land in this area sold by William Penn, and anecdotes about George and Martha Washington's visit there are still recounted, it is clear that this place is uniquely significant in the history of New Hope.

Part of the estate is known as Maple Grove. It has more history and tradition attached to it than probably any other homestead in Bucks County. Maple Grove and its older counterpart, Northwood Farms, constitute what is today as the Rhoads Estate in New Hope. Joseph Pike obtained the six hundred and twenty-four acres from William Penn in 1705, and shortly afterward obtained the area's first fishing license from Penn. The acreage was so vast that it encompassed the area from Sugan Road on the west to the Delaware River on the east and ran north to Rabbit's Run and south to what is now Bridge Street. Thomas Paxson purchased the land from Pike's heirs about sixty years later. The Paxson, Ely and Rhoads families have owned a large portion of that land intermittently for two and a half centuries to the present time.

Maple Grove—the Paxson-Rhoads House

> **When ten generations of a family continue to occupy land that was the largest tract of land in this area sold by William Penn, and anecdotes about George and Martha Washington's visit there are still recounted, it is clear that this place is uniquely significant in the history of New Hope.**

Maple Grove located at 102 West Bridge Street was built for Ruthanna Paxson Ely and her sister, Margaret Paxson Rhoads. It is one of two buildings remaining on the site that was, after Brigadier General Roche de Fermoy selected the site, General William Alexander's encampment for three weeks prior to the Battle of Trenton in 1776. Then, in 1778, it was included in the area of General George Washington's Continental Army bivouac on its way from Valley Forge to the Battle of Monmouth in New Jersey.

One legend has it that when General George Washington was asked by his wife, Martha, what she should do if she should encounter General Howe, George responded that she should wear one of Mrs. Paxson's Quaker dresses and she would be completely safe from the flirtatious general. This was undoubtedly a reference to the Paxsons frugality, hard work, sense of values and simplicity. Another version of the story substitutes Mrs. Paxson's Quaker bonnet for the dress.

Northwood Farm, a stately fieldstone farmhouse, occupies the northern part of the homestead. It may have been built around 1760 by Thomas Paxson, Sr. Of great additional interest to New Hope's history, the home was willed to his son Oliver Paxson, the father of Jane Paxson Parry. Jane was the wife of Benjamin Parry, widely considered to be the "father" of New Hope for his great community involvement and entrepreneurship that succeeded in putting New Hope on the map in the late eighteenth and early nineteenth centuries. The home was moved a short distance to its present location several years ago when it had undergone a marvelous renovation by the Rhoads family. This great farmhouse in its renovated splendor can be clearly seen from Hardy Bush Way, the back road into New Hope from Route 202.

The Parry Mansion—1784

The construction of this fine center hall Georgian style home was probably begun in the early 1780's and completed in 1787 by Benjamin Parry. He had purchased the mill from Dr. Joseph Todd's widow and may have purchased this house as part of that transaction. Parry was a third generation Welsh Quaker who was descended from a very old and honorable family in North Wales, England. The original part of his house was constructed with blue field stone from nearby quarries. More readily available red field stone was used to construct the kitchen addition that also housed the servants. Architect and historian, Margaret Bye Richie, called the Parry Mansion one of New Hope's three most significant houses. She includes the home with Springdale and Cintra, homes that are also discussed in this publication.

The Parry Mansion in 1960

About one hundred and seventy-three years after Benjamin Parry moved into his spanking new 1787 mansion on 45 South Main Street with his blushing new bride, Jane Paxson Parry, his great, great granddaughter, Margaret Parry Lang moved into the home with her husband, Oliver Paul Lang. She had inherited the house from her aunt Adelaide Parry following her death in 1958. She, thus, became the fifth consecutive generation of the Parry Family to live in the mansion. And each generation had its own ideas about how the home should be decorated.

Mrs. Lang told the Philadelphia *Sunday Bulletin*, in a story published in June, 1960, that she had been born in the Parry Mansion, but had moved away at an early age. Returning to the elegant house brought old memories flowing back. She remembered that the house had once been furnished totally with colonial pieces. But what she found in the ten-room mansion was mostly Victorian. So, with the help of local contractor, Edwin Scarborough and interior decorator, Ruth Page, she set about changing the Victorian-era décor back to the colonial charm that she had remembered from her childhood days. Mrs. Lang related that she found all of the old colonial pieces of furniture and décor in the attic. "No Parry ever threw anything away," she proudly told the reporter.

> **With the help and guidance of noted designer, Charles Lamar, the Historical Society completed a full scale renovation of the (Parry) mansion.**

Just eight years later Margaret Parry Lang and her husband sold the Parry Mansion to the New Hope Historical Society. They also auctioned off most of the furniture. It was closed for seven years while the Historical Society planned yet another design for Benjamin Parry's home. With the help and guidance of noted designer, Charles Lamar, the Historical Society completed a full-scale renovation of the mansion creating a veritable museum of art, furniture and design representing five periods of history ranging from 1775 to 1900.

The George Ely House—c. 1795

Known for decades as "The Pink House," a popular emporium for those seeking precious items from the distant past, the George Ely House on 80 West Ferry Street presents an excellent example of the way that properties in early New Hope changed hands.

George Ely, grandfather of Hiram Ely, whose home is located just down the street, and will be discussed in later in this publication, purchased the tract from Oliver Paxson, the father-in-law of Benjamin Parry. The house appears on Parry's map that he had drawn up in 1798. This ranks the George Ely House as one of the five oldest homes remaining in New Hope. Just about fifty years later the home was purchased by Oliver Parry, the only son of Benjamin Parry. Real estate transactions among relatives in early New Hope were numerous, moving from one side of the family to the other with amazing frequency. Oliver Parry and his wife, Rachel Randolph, had also purchased the home directly across the street at 89 West Ferry Street.

The George Ely House in 2008

Although the George Ely House faces south, fronting on West Ferry Street, there is also frontage on West Bridge Street which had been built at the time when the first bridge from New Hope to Lambertville had been built under the supervision of, none other than, Benjamin Parry around 1814. Various owners of the home over the years have used either of the streets as their addresses.

The George Ely House is located on the Old York Road which has been incorporated into West Ferry Street. Over the past century and a half the structural integrity of the house has suffered from awkward additions such as sheds and chimneys. Recent renovations to the house, however, have handsomely cleaned up and meticulously renovated the property exposing a portion of the old fieldstone section of the rear of the home that is now visible from West Bridge Street.

The John Beaumont House—c. 1791

Not a lot of folks know about New Hope's "pentagon" partially hidden under the West Ferry Street canal bridge. It is not a government top secret compound. It's just that it is very difficult to see that the John Beaumont House located at 21 W. Ferry Street is five-sided. This odd construction design was not planned, but rather evolved over the course of the past two hundred years or so as the face of New Hope was changed by the construction of the Delaware Canal in the late 1820's.

The Beaumont House is located on land that once included the property purchased by Benjamin Parry from John Beaumont to build his elegant Parry Mansion just down the street. He had acquired about 72 acres in a sheriff sale of John Coryell's holdings in 1785. Beaumont was a wealthy gentleman who owned a large amount of real estate at the time. He was the father-in-law of William Maris, a major competitor of Benjamin Parry. Beaumont built the impressive federal style house we see today.

The John Beaumont House

Beaumont leased the property to Garrret Meldrum, a noted New Hope entrepreneur, who eventually purchased the property and added a tavern. Interestingly, Benjamin Parry was an appraiser of Meldrum's estate when he died in 1819. When the Delaware Canal was built through New Hope around 1830 the house was changed forever. A portion of the old Hatter Shop was removed to make way for the canal construction leaving the structure with only five sides remaining—thus, the "pentagon". Adding insult to injury Ferry Street was raised thereby creating a rather steep hill directly in front of the main entrance to the home. So, if you ever wondered why someone would build such a beautiful home, partially under a bridge—they didn't. The canal bridge came later.

The main part of the Beaumont House is a fine example of the Georgian style in the Federal period around 1800. The geometric patterns in the stone are fascinating. The original stone chimneys have been replaced with brick. Six fire places and a walk-in fire place in the kitchen add to the splendid charm of this architectural treasure.

New Hope owes much to the work and dedication of Sally Goodman who restored much of this house to its original splendor in the mid 1970's after it had been steadily deteriorating for more than half a century. Earlier, John Byer and Bernard Robin had begun alterations on the house. Sally Goodman's Antiques has been housed there for the past three decades.

The Poor-Ely House—c. 1795

The John Poor-Cornelius Ely House located at 91 West Ferry Street has been acclaimed by architect and historian, Margaret Bye Richie, who wrote that "The entire house has the stamp of integrity written into its lines and treatment; one suspects that it has been scarcely touched since the early nineteenth century."

This property has been traced as far back as 1745 when it came into the hands of Benjamin Canby, the second operator of the ferry and for whom New Hope was once named, "Canby's Ferry."

During the American Revolutionary War this property was part of the site of major encampments for General George Washington's army.

John Poor and Robert Neely purchased the property in 1798 and may have built the older part of the house on the site of an old saw mill. About ten years later, John and Cornelius Ely leased the property and built the dwelling. Cornelius Ely, a lumber merchant, purchased the house in 1816 and it remained in his family until his death in 1835.

The John Poor-Cornelius Ely House

This two thirds Georgian style house was included on Benjamin Parry's map of 1798. Ironically, it was owned at one time by Major Edward Randolph, the father-in-law of Oliver Parry, Benjamin Parry's only son. Oliver and his wife, Rachel, eventually bought the house in 1846.

The main entrance to the house has an arched Georgian style framing with a narrow peaked gable. Today the house is owned by Richard and Ruth Hirschfield and remains as one of New Hope's most outstanding early dwellings.

The Osmond-Newhart House—c. 1795

The beautiful two and a half story and plaster over fieldstone, double structure located at 75-77 West Ferry Street is documented on the map created by Benjamin Parry in 1798 designated as the House of J. Osmond.

The house has seen many transformations and several additions since the days when it saw countless stage coaches rumble in front of it on their way from Philadelphia to Manhattan. West Ferry Street, originally York Road, was one of the oldest stage coach routes on the east coast.

It is believed that the house was built by Jonathan Osmond just before the turn of the nineteenth century. Over the past two hundred and ten years ownership of the house has changed numerous times going from Osmond to John Poor and on to the Ely, Maris, Beaumont, Phillips, Umpleby, Slaughter and, more recently, to the Newhart family.

The Osmond-Newhart House in 2008

For nearly sixty years until about 1925 the Osmond/Newhart House was a provisions store supplying the daily needs of the families who worked in the Lepanto Mills. The mills, which produced flax, had been located between the Osmond House and Ingham Creek, just around the corner, and were owned by William Maris. More than eighty years ago the store window was removed and the kitchen door was changed to a window. Looking at the house from the front on the West Ferry Street side, one can quickly see the similarities in appearance to the Farley's Book Shop building just a couple of blocks way at 44 South Main Street.

Today a beautiful mural reminiscent of New Hope artist Joseph Pickett's famous "billboard" size paintings of this area can be seen on the east side of the house.

Stone Row—c.1789

New Hope entrepreneur, John Beaumont, built the housing now known as "Stone Row" on 61 through 71 West Ferry Street in the late

1780's to provide housing for local mill workers. He certainly never dreamed that nearly two centuries later they would become fancy accommodations for actors from New York playing at St. John Terrell's Music Festival in Lambertville, New Jersey or at the Bucks County Playhouse. Where once the exhausted mill workers found refuge after a hard day's labor at the local flax and silk mills, actors like Helen Hayes, Ann Miller, Tom Poston, Robert Redford, Martha Raye and Imogene Coca partied while staying in New Hope during some of their early theatrical appearances nearly a century later.

"Regents Row" painting by Marsha McCort--1982

These six dwellings were built as "company houses" for employees of New Hope's early mill industry. They had interlocking deeds until as recently as 1972. Each house is now separately deeded and privately owned. When companies no longer felt obligated to provide housing for their workers, the eighteenth century stone houses steadily deteriorated to the point that they had become the borough's slums by 1900.

These beautiful colonial fieldstone homes were purchased by the Doylestown Trust through a corporation known as "Stone Row, Inc." headed by Pamela Minford, and once again became rental housing in the early 1960's. A few years later they were magnificently restored by Charles and Nancy Eaton. Much of the original wood was preserved including the random width oak floors as have all of the charming closed circular stairs. All of the old "out houses" were torn down, and each unit was enlarged on the south side of the buildings to provide a dining room, den and modern baths. A porch was added to the third floors. The Eaton Family built an additional house on the east side of the structure for their personal use.

"Stone Row" or "Regents Row" as it once had been named is located on West Ferry Street. That was part of the Old York Road, one of the oldest stage coach routes on the east coast. It connected Philadelphia with New York and was the regular route of the Swift Sure State Coach Company that brought business and tourist travelers to New Hope, the half way point of the two-day journey. And long before that time the Lenni-Lenape had cut the trail on their seasonal journeys between Philadelphia and New Hope.

Original ownership of the land has been traced to James Logan, secretary to William Penn. Over the years a number of prominent New Hope wheelers and dealers such as Coryell, Beaumont, Parry, Maris, Doan, Magill and Ely have owned the property at one time or another.

The fortunate residents of "Stone Row" today can savor the rich history of their neighborhood from the original settlers, the Lenni-Lenape, to the mill workers and to classic stars of stage and screen. The borough of New Hope is currently constructing a neighborhood park directly across the street that will be appropriately named "Lenape Park" to commemorate the original settlers of New Hope nearly ten thousand years ago.

The Jane Magill House—c. 1798

John Magill is believed to have built the original section of this grand fieldstone structure above Old York Road and Sugan Road in the late 1790's and bequeathed it to his daughters, Jane and Rachel Magill in 1812. This two and a half story single family dwelling was part of Springdale, the mini-village on the western side of the borough that gave rise to the mill industry in New Hope in the early eighteenth century. It was once home to employees of the cotton and grist mills that were located nearby.

Close observation of the home reveals that it had been built in two sections. There are two front entrance doors. The west side is the older section and was constructed with fieldstone and, although it is the lowest level it is situated slightly above grade due to its location on the lower level of the terrain. Quarry stone was used in building the newer, east side of the home. Ann Niessen, in her study of the home in 1980, pointed out that the Jane Magill House has one of the oldest remaining Bucks County stone bridges located near its front door with an inscription, "Sugan Bridge 1853."

The Jane Magill House

The house has been standing guard over the southwest corner of Old York Road and South Sugan Road for nearly two centuries from the time that stage coaches rumbled along on their way from Philadelphia to New York City, stopping by New Hope for an overnight's rest. The property was originally owned by Samuel Jones, and has had numerous owners over the years. It had been in the Zinger family for more than fifty years until it was recently sold.

Unfortunately, the grand old house now stands empty and appears isolated compared to the old days of the mill workers, stage coaches and merchants who once made the Jane Magill house a centerpiece of their activities.

Willow Brook—c.1800

Motorists ramble along Sugan Road behind a convenience store barely catching a glimpse of one of the most charming little cottages in Bucks County. There on the southwest corner of South Sugan Road and Old York Road stands the beautiful two and a half story fieldstone dwelling covered with an ochre-colored sand plaster known as The John Magill House and nicknamed "Willow Brook."

This charming, unpretentious home was probably built by John Magill around 1800. The Magill family is one of the oldest in the New Hope area of Bucks County and is still prominent in the community today. The house was probably built to provide a dwelling for some of the workers who were employed at the old Heath grist mill and Maris cotton mill that had been located just around the bend on the west side of Sugan Road. The ruins of the Maris mill can still be seen today as they have been reconstructed for residential use.

Willow Brook

Willow Brook was one of about twenty buildings that comprised a kind of "mini village" on the western side of New Hope from the early 1700's until the late 1800's. In fact, the little village once had its own toll booth situated diagonally across the road from Willow Brook. Ann Niessen's research of the property in 1978 indicated that more than one hundred years ago, there were twenty-one single family homes located in the little village. And, as she had indicated thirty years ago, the intersection of Old York Road and South Sugan Road still remains virtually as they had appeared nearly two hundred years ago.

The parcel of land on which this gorgeous dwelling was constructed had previously been owned by the famous, Andrew Ellicott, who, among many other accomplishments, was summoned by Congress to design the nation's capital when Pierre Charles L'Enfant resigned from the commission taking the plans for Washington, D.C. with him. When Thomas Canby purchased the land from Jacob Holcombe in 1717, it still contained Robert Heath's original mill which has now long-since disappeared.

The Stockton-Turner House—c. 1798

The original part of the Stockton-Turner house located at 54 West Ferry Street dates as far back as Benjamin Parry's early map of New Hope drawn in 1798. It may have been owned for a short time by Parry before it was sold to Cephas Ross, an early New Hope community activist. It is one of four frame houses on West Ferry Street facing south on what was the originally part of York Road.

About two-thirds of the structure was originally an eighteenth century Georgian style house that was built shortly after the Parry Mansion, just about one block east on Ferry Street. About a century later additions modified the three-gable, double pile house with an entry porch and bay, and a building at the rear of the house facing Bridge Street.

The Stockton-Turner House

Like many other houses and buildings in New Hope the Stockton-Turner House was once owned, although briefly by Lewis S. Coryell, before losing it at a sheriff's sale. Although there were a number of other owners, Joseph P. Stockton, one of the directors of the New Hope-Lambertville Bridge Company after it was partially destroyed by a flood in 1841, was the owner for nearly eighty years. His daughter, Helen Stockton, bequeathed the house to the New Hope Methodist Episcopal Church in 1937. But the church quickly sold it to Dr. Henry W. Turner and his wife, Mary. Interestingly enough, according to historian, Margaret Bye Richie, Dr. Turner was a veterinarian who practiced with a circus and his wife was a horseback rider with that same circus. She was also an illustrator of children's books. Mary lived in the house until it was sold to noted New Hope antiques dealer and active citizen, George Hobensack in 1963. Today it is home to New Hope's mayor, Laurence D. Keller, proprietor of Hobensack and Keller Antiques. It has recently undergone extensive renovations and has been beautifully landscaped. The Stockton-Turner House today, beautifully restored and preserved, represents a magnificent blend of eighteenth and nineteenth century architecture.

Cintra—1824

On a trip abroad, New Hope entrepreneur, William Maris, became enchanted by a palace in Cintra, Portugal located about seventeen miles west-northwest of Lisbon. When he returned home he began construction of what is still known as "Cintra" around 1824. It is interesting to note that his massive Lepanto Mills project which has been discussed earlier was just nearing completion when Maris began the construction of Cintra. His New Hope "palace" emulates a section of its counterpart in Portugal. It is a two and a half story fieldstone house with thick walls that are covered with yellow pebble dash. It is buttressed by two wings at its northeast and northwest levels. The rear elevation of this hub, in addition to the southeast and southwest elevations are another full story above grade creating perfect symmetry and proportion. This great residence is fan-shaped similar to the Octagon in Washington, D.C.

The Royal Palace at Cintra, Portugal

The interior of Cintra is mansion-like in every way. The front door leads into an entrance hall that is an oblong, octagonal shape. . Doors open to the parlor on the left and the dining room on the right. Opposite the front door, another set of double doors leads into a hall eight feet wide that extends through the house. On the second floor is a spacious octagonal bedroom is nestled over the entrance hall. The library and pantry are located off the rear of the hall, and a door in the center of the hall provides access to the magnificent piazza in the rear of the house. Four large bedrooms are located on the second floor.

Alas, William Maris's numerous ventures in the building and manufacturing trades led to his financial undoing. The great dream that he realized in Cintra became the taunting joke among townspeople as "Maris's Folly." It was a short-lived dream that ended less than three years after he had occupied his grand residence. After losing most of his holdings at sheriff's sales Maris returned to Philadelphia around 1834 and died there shortly afterward. His legacy endures today in the grand buildings that he created in the New Hope community.

Maris's "Cintra" in New Hope

Cintra remained in the prominent Ely Family for more than one hundred years after Maris had departed. The gracious residence has long been the site of the prestigious Joseph Stanley period English furniture shop.

The Joseph Pickett House—c.1829

If you are a relatively unknown artist who is seeking recognition, what better way to get a attention from the public than by painting your work on the side of your building—especially if it is a very large building situated on the most popular street for art lovers? This practice went from the sublime to the profane in the 1960's when "Bull Durham" tobacco advertised on the east wall of the building. The photo on the following page shows the house at is it appears today.

Long after it was the home of mechanics who labored at the nearby mills in New Hope, West Mechanic Street became known as the "Latin Quarter of New Hope." This charming, colorful street is still the favorite of many visitors and residents alike. It seems to have the feel of a Rue Moufetard in Paris or even a small by-way in Greenwich Village.

The Joseph Pickett House in 2008

Pickett may have spent too much of his time painting and too little working in the store, much to the chagrin of his wife, Emily, who is said to have sold or destroyed most of his remaining paintings after his death because she claimed that she had no room for them in the house.

The Pickett House was built around 1829, just before the Delaware Canal was constructed in New Hope. It is located on land that was once part of the Joshua Van Sant plantation. The property changed hands numerous times. In the early 1890's Joseph Pickett opened a general store in the building. He painted his works in the back room. It is believed that his best known work, "Manchester Valley," was completed in that room. His billboard size paintings on the exterior walls of the building that had delighted his generation were, unfortunately, destroyed when the building was whitewashed not long after Pickett died.

The Joshua Whiteley House—1855

Simon Gove built the house around 1855 to provide lodging for the workers at the nearby mills, and there have been more than twenty owners of the homestead over the past one hundred and fifty years.

But through the past one and a half centuries and the scores of residents who have called it home, this magnificent two and a half story clapboard structure atop the Ingham Creek on South Sugar Road continues to be known as the Joshua Whiteley House.

Joshua Whiteley was born in Yorkshire, England in 1823. As a youth he learned the skill for manufacturing woolen cloths. When he was thirty years old Joshua arrived in the United States and settled in Upper Darby, Pennsylvania. In just a few years he and his brothers, Joseph and John, formed a partnership with John Ashworth to create a firm known as Whiteley Brothers & Company that quite successfully manufactured cotton and woolen goods along Cobbs Creek in Delaware County.

In 1856 Joshua married Catherine Buckley. They had five children. After Catherine died following a prolonged illness in 1869, Joshua married her younger sister, Lavina, and they brought thirteen children into the New Hope world. One of the children, Kate, was a teacher at the old school on the hill.

The Joshua Whiteley House in 2008

His drive and entrepreneurship led Whiteley to sell his interest in the company after about eight years when he came to New Hope in 1864 and purchased the old William Maris cotton mills, the house and a portion of land from John Bouman for $19,000. It is reported in the

History of Bucks County that Joshua Whiteley began to manufacture cotton warp in 1865. Under his shrewd management his business became one of the leading industries in New Hope and created employment for nearly fifty people. It is reported that Whiteley's mill turned out nearly 4,500 pounds of yarn per week. Whiteley continued to own the property until around 1895, some thirty years after beginning his venture in New Hope. It is said that Mr. Whiteley never recovered from the loss of his mill. It was converted into a silk mill around 1898, and closed permanently in 1930. Joshua Whiteley died in 1909. He and many of his family members are buried in the Holcombe Riverview Cemetery in Lambertville, New Jersey.

Later, the Joshua Whiteley House had been home to New Hope artist, Bill Nye, who sold it to Eleanor Pollock Hughes, editor of the Women's Page for the Philadelphia Bulletin newspaper, who owned the house from the early 1940's to the early 1960's. She had worked with President Lyndon Johnson in the White House. Ms. Pollock Hughes was a close friend of UPI press correspondent, Helen Thomas, who was a frequent visitor to the house. The interior and exterior of the house were completely restored and returned to a single-family dwelling in the early 1990's by John Pallatinus and Jack Alexander. The house is now owned by Joe Knox, vice president of the New Hope Historical Society and Constable, Rick Sweeney.

CHAPTER 5

New Hope in the Revolutionary War

New Hope's greatest claim to historical significance occurred in June, 1778. General George Washington with about 10,000 troops of the Continental Army, nearly 1,000 horses and wagons, artillery and baggage marched from Valley Forge, Pennsylvania to the pivotal Battle of Monmouth in New Jersey. They camped for three days in New Hope, then Coryell's Ferry, and crossed at the ferry landing to New Jersey. This spectacular event occurred over three days: June 20, 21 and 22 in 1778. Coryell's Ferry was also an important site from which Washington's troops conducted reconnaissance missions and had bivouacked on their way to the fateful Battle of Trenton in 1776 that turned the course of the Revolutionary War.

Washington Crossing Re-enactment by the Coryell's Ferry Militia

Today, with nearly three centuries of rich history, the Ferry Landing Park where General Washington had crossed, hosts thousands of visitors and residents providing a spectacular view of the Delaware River and historic markers that tell of its great history.

> **New Hope's greatest claim to historical significance (in the Revolutionary War) occurred in June, 1778. General George Washington with about 10,000 troops of the Continental Army…marched from Valley Forge, Pennsylvania to the pivotal Battle of Monmouth in New Jersey and…camped for three days in New Hope.**

Each December, the Coryell's Ferry Militia Re-enactment group annually portrays the history of General William Washington and Colonel James Monroe's crossing that reportedly occurred in Coryell's Ferry a week or so prior to General George Washington's crossing at McConkey's Ferry about seven miles south of New Hope in 1776. In June, in conjunction with the New Hope Historical Society's annual New Hope History Day, the re-enactors also commemorate George Washington's crossing in New Hope in 1778.

The Wedgwood Inn

Twenty-first century guests who seek lodging at the award-winning Wedgwood Inn Bed and Breakfast receive an extra bonus during their stays there. They are rewarded with an ambience steeped in American history that few other inns in this area can provide. The innkeepers have taken great care in decorating various rooms within the popular get-away spot with photographs, news stories and documents about the location's strategic place in American history.

The Wedgwood Inn

The elegant, clapboard structure was built around 1870 by Maryann Slaughter on the foundation of the "Old Fort," the "old hip roof house" built around 1720 to which the prominent historian, W.W. H. Davis, had referred in his *History of Bucks County*. It was the site of the fort where General Alexander, also known as Lord Stirling, made his headquarters during the two weeks prior to the Battle of Trenton in December, 1776. Correspondence indicates the Generals Monroe and Madison had also stayed on the site at one time or another while plans for the Battle of Trenton were being formulated. About 1,200 troops bivouacked in the area just across the street from the Wedgwood Inn.

When the inn was renovated around 1990, a tunnel was discovered that is believed to have served as an ammunitions storage facility for the Continental Army in the eighteenth century. The remains of a Hessian soldier, who, perhaps, had fled during the war, were found with gold buttons from his uniform, trapped in the chimney of a walk-in fireplace in the basement.

Another intriguing theory suggests that part of the tunnel has been used as a section of the Underground Railroad to assist escaping slaves in the nineteenth century. A fascinating glimpse of the tunnel can be viewed outside the dining area at the inn. A secret stairway that leads to the tunnel adds to the excitement of a stay at the Wedgwood Inn.

The keen interest demonstrated by Carl and Nadine Glassman, owners of the inn, for New Hope's place in American history over the past three centuries and there infectious enthusiasm about it is a great tribute to them. It adds to the rich appreciation of New Hope's vast historic importance to the many hundreds of visitors who stay at the inn more than two centuries after famous generals plotted battle strategies and took refuge there during the American Revolution.

CHAPTER 6

Transportation

The Ferry Landing

The earliest recorded use of the Ferry Landing on the Delaware River in New Hope was the acquisition of a license to keep a ferry operation there by John Wells around 1718. He was a carpenter and is said to have constructed the ferry operations at considerable expense. In addition to operating the first ferry, Wells was licensed to open the first tavern. Wells is considered to be the "founder" of New Hope which, from 1717 to 1747, bore the name "Wells Ferry."

The Ferry Landing in 1909

45

Native Americans had, undoubtedly, used the site of the ferry landing for river crossings for many centuries before John Wells arrived on the scene. Following Wells, the ferry operations were owned by Benjamin Canby and John Coryell before being acquired by Benjamin Parry around 1814.

Ferry operations continued across the Delaware River from New Hope to Lambertville which, during the time of Washington's crossing, had both been named Coryell's Ferry, until about 1818. Benjamin Parry had received authorization from the State Legislature to purchase the ferry operations in 1811 and, with his partners, obtained permission to build a bridge to Lambertville, New Jersey. Shortly after the bridge was constructed and opened in 1816, the ferry operations ceased.

Until the completion of the Delaware Canal, Durham boats, rafts and arks were the only means of transport along the river to Philadelphia. The last Durham boat is said to have completed the trip in 1865. The floods of 1903 and 1955 brought massive devastation to the area.

By 1811, Benjamin Parry had become the principal entrepreneur in New Hope, then called Coryell's Ferry. Undoubtedly, the cost of transporting his flour, oil, produce and meat products to markets in New Jersey and New York was considerable. So, it is understandable that Parry saw the great benefits that he could reap, if he could gain control of the ferry rights and build a toll bridge to Lambertville which, at that time, had also been named Coryell's Ferry. His goods and those of other local merchants could then be hauled to New York with Parry and his partners reaping the benefits of the toll collections.

The New Hope-Lambertville Bridge

Parry and his friend and business partner, Samuel Ingham, were the driving forces that obtained authorization from the state legislature to become the commission to supervise the construction of the bridge that led to the formation of the New Hope Delaware Bridge Company in 1811. Construction began in the following year on the covered bridge with six spans about 1,050 feet long. By the time the bridge was completed in 1814 at a cost of about $68,000 including ferry rights and toll houses, the town on the New Jersey side of the river had already been changed to Lambertville. It would be another twenty-three years until New Hope was incorporated. Just four years later the flood of 1841 carried away three spans. At least two owners followed Parry and Ingham's stewardship of the bridge. After the flood of 1903, the bridge was rebuilt with steel and re-opened in 1904. Finally, in 1910 it was taken over by the Joint Bridge Commission at a cost of about $225,000.

Construction of the new bridge in 1904

The bridge we see today is supported by caissons that were used to build the original span. The steel bridge had been severely damaged by the great flood of 1955 that took about a month to repair. Just recently the bridge was fortified and repainted, and now serves the thousands of motorists and pedestrians that use it every day.

Times have changed. No longer is there a fine of five dollars for driving or riding across the bridge faster than a pedestrian could walk; or for taking more than ten horses at a time; or for smoking or carrying lighted cigars or pipes across the bridge or for crossing without paying a toll. But the fine for driving over the fifteen mile per hour speed limit today will set you back many times that amount—with or without horses!

The Delaware Canal

The year 1826, was not a good one for Benjamin Parry, the New Hope entrepreneur who had put the town on the industrial map. Parry had lost the love of his life, Jane Paxson Parry, who died at the early age of fifty-nine years. Later that year New Hope's first bank, which he and his partners had opened, failed; and they were forced to sell it. But Parry's Quaker faith rooted him in times of despair and gave him the hope and determination to go on after his latest crisis. In the following year the Delaware Canal was authorized by the state, and, shortly afterward, Parry, like many other industrialists and farmers, played a significant role in the financing of the construction of the canal through New Hope.

The Delaware Canal in New Hope—1915

As the Industrial Revolution continued to demand vast amounts of resources the need to transport coal and other materials from upstate Pennsylvania to Philadelphia and New York City became urgent giving rise to one of our nation's most amazing engineering feats. At its peak the Delaware Canal carried 3,000 canal boats each year through New Hope and on to the cities. Boatmen's work days were long beginning at sunrise and often lasting until late in the evening. It is reported that, at its peak year of operation in 1866, the Delaware Canal was the conduit for 792,000 tons of anthracite coal, alone, that had been shipped from

Carbon County, Pennsylvania. New Hope was the central point of the Delaware Canal between Easton and Bristol, Pennsylvania. Canal boats heading for New Jersey and New York entered a feeder canal near Odette's River House Restaurant. They were hooked to a cable and pulled across the Delaware River to the Delaware-Raritan Canal and from there navigated there way north. Other canal boats going to Philadelphia proceeded south on the Pennsylvania side of the river to Bristol.

But, even from the early years, the canal was used as a place for recreational activities. Marion Oblinger Cooper was born in 1886 and lived in what is now known as Stone Row on West Ferry Street. They were friends of the Parry family. Her daughter, Edna Cooper, had revealed a section of Marion's diary that told of the great pleasures that folks experienced from the canal in the nineteenth century. "And the skating parties. The canal was wonderful for miles, but our limit was to Lumberville and return. We glided across the snow four or five in a row clasping hands in front of us and feeling the rhythm of our swinging bodies and only hearing the glide of the sharp skates. We'd leave the moonlit canal sadly, but so tired sometimes we could hardly walk." And in the summer she remembers; "Again crossing of the river from the island and the stepping stones to the towpath and the waiting scowl on the canal. Baskets were uncovered again and supper was in progress. After being satisfied, all began to sing and we came down the canal calling to the people living along the towpath. At last we docked, tired, but so happy." Edna Cooper added that her grandmother often talked about life on the canal and how, as children, they played at the canal and the children would be there all day.

> **At its peak the Delaware Canal carried 3,000 canal boats through New Hope and on to markets in Philadelphia and New York City.**

Today the Delaware Canal in Pennsylvania is one of the most expansive recreational areas in the United States offering nearly sixty miles of wooded land along the scenic and historic Delaware River from Easton to Bristol. Due to the nature of its construction, the canal has always been fragile and frequently has sustained serious damage and deterioration. Over the past fifty years or so volunteer organizations like the Delaware Valley Protective Association and more recently the Friends of the Delaware Canal were formed to augment the state's efforts to preserve and maintain the canal. They have been instrumental in keeping this great historic waterway alive so that the thousands who walk, hike, picnic, bike, run or tour along the towpath today can enjoy the same kind of great pleasure as those experienced by Edna Cooper's family nearly one hundred and fifty years ago.

The New Hope-Ivyland Railroad Station

The old New Hope Train Station of the Reading Company line that had been serving New Hope since 1891 had been literally put out to pasture in 1954, just two years after the last train left the station. It was relocated to a field about a few thousand yards behind its original location and was to be used by a local sportsmen's club. Again, it was the hard work and fundraising activities of the Historical Society's board of directors and members with support from the New Hope community that made this effort possible. The top of the cone-shaped turret had been damaged, but the rail station at Wycombe was used as a model to restore the New Hope station.

New Hope Rail Station in 2008

So, in 1966, a dozen years after the rail station had been deteriorating out in the woods, the Historical Society brought it back to New Hope and restored it to pristine condition, thus preserving another historic landmark.

The New Hope Trolleys

The first trolley cars in Bucks County started in 1897 in Newtown. Gradually, as their popularity increased, routes were opened from Doylestown to Willow Grove and another to Newtown. In retrospect, the network that emerged is truly remarkable. Trolley routes wound their way from Quakertown to Richlandtown and from Perkasie to Lansdale. The old "Liberty Bell" route was so extensive that it included communities from Zion Hill and Sellersville through Quakertown and all the way to Allentown and back to Philadelphia. That route experienced great financial success through its freight service as well as passenger rides and survived until 1951

The New Hope borough council passed an ordinance in June, 1904 authorizing trolley service to the borough, and on July 23, 1905 the first "street railroad" car, as they were once called, made its maiden voyage from Trenton, New Jersey to New Hope and on to Lambertville.

It was a rough journey of about eleven miles that crossed the Calhoun Street Bridge from Trenton to Morrisville and continued on through fields and farms from Yardley to Washington's Crossing, Brownsburg (where a power station was located), Upper Makefield and finally arriving in New Hope about an hour later.

The New Hope Trolley entering Lambertville in 1923

Passenger trolleys were scheduled every hour from six o'clock in the morning until midnight. The initial cost of a ride from Lambertville to Trenton was twenty-five cents, but was quickly raised to thirty and then to thirty-five cents. Regardless, the trolley remained a popular way to travel for eighteen years. The New Hope, Lambertville, Trenton route crossed the Delaware River over the Calhoun Street Bridge. There was a trolley terminal located on Hanover and Warren Streets in Trenton. That was the main terminal where all central New Jersey lines connected. Freight service was provided once a day. New Hopians could ride to Philadelphia on the trolley by connecting at Morrisville and Bristol.

An early rider described the ride as "swaying and jammed" and heated by a pot-bellied stove. Others, recalls John Richardson, complained that the ride was a "bumpy and travel-sickening adventure. Yet, with all of that discomfort, the trolley remained a popular mode of travel for eighteen years in New Hope. America's love affair with the automobile coupled with the continued increases in fares spelled the end of a curious relationship and the trolley made its last run through New Hope in October, 1923.

Eighty-five years later, the trolley returned to New Hope. The Bucks County Riverboat and Trolley Company began its new tours of the New Hope area on August 9, 2008. The new trolleys provided a comfortable ride over part of the same route that the original "street railroad" car traversed in 1905. But that trolley rode on four wheels instead of one rail. The twenty-first century version of the old trolley began its ninety-minute tour at the Parry Mansion on the corner of West Ferry and South Main Streets in New Hope. The route traveled south, pointing out historic buildings and sites along the way. Riders were taken along the old trolley route to Washington's Crossing Historic Park for a self-guided tour followed by a journey to the top of Bowman's Hill for the most spectacular view in Bucks County. The old trolley could never have negotiated that hill. The tour wound through Aquetong Road to the historic Springdale section and down the Old York Road back to New Hope.

CHAPTER 7

The New Hope Historical Society

Dr. Arthur J. Ricker was elected first president of the New Hope Historical Society in 1958 by members who had been meeting almost every day over lunch at the Logan Inn to discuss the rich art, culture and historical legacy of the borough. It is situated on about 1,000 acres of stunning landscape that has inspired world renowned artists for generations. It is also the strategic place selected by General George Washington to stage the preparations for the fateful Battle of Trenton and the march to the Battle of Monmouth.

Mindful of this rich legacy the Historical Society's board of directors set out to preserve it for generations to come. They began with the purchase of the eighteenth century Parry Barn in 1958 that, at the time, seemed destined for demolition and reincarnation as a modern, glitzy diner. They preserved the exterior in its original state and transformed the interior of the barn into an art gallery, lecture hall and museum to display relics of the past. The great Pennsylvania Impressionist, Edward Redfield, lectured there in the 1960's.Just recently, the Parry Barn was the focus of art lovers around the region as it hosted the popular Bucks County artist, Joseph Crilley, for his annual art exhibit and sale.

Dr. Arthur J. Ricker, left, forms the Historical Society

Dr. Ricker and his original board envisioned a kind of "mini-Williamsburg" that would include the preservation of buildings included within the boundaries of Ferry Street and Mechanic Street from the Delaware River to the Delaware Canal.

Official New Hope Historic Stamp—1958

A variety of fundraisers helped to pay for the costs of purchase and renovations. The Historical Society, with the help of artist, Alden Wicks, designed an Official New Hope Historical stamp that was sold in all New Hope shops. In 1958 and 1959 they sold 120,000 stamps. The first arts and crafts show and an antiques show continued the effort in 1960. The fundraising efforts made possible the historic preservation of the Parry Barn.

Original Historic Site markers Placed in 1966

The eighteenth century Parry Barn that is reputed to have housed some of General Washington's horses during the Revolutionary War became an endangered species, so to speak, around 1960 when plans for its demolition and replacement with a modern diner were being formulated. Dr. Ricker rallied his board, securing a loan to purchase the structure.

Following the purchase of the Parry Barn the Historical Society set out to preserve the exterior of the barn and to transform the interior space into a beautiful art gallery, lecture hall and museum. Eventually the board of directors decided to rent the Parry Barn in order to raise funds for their next purchase—the Parry Mansion. The Golden Door Gallery was opened by Nancy Shaw and then was operated by Mary Gardner for thirty-four years providing a venue for new works by area artists.

Eighteenth Century Parry Barn saved in 1958

The generosity of the New Hope area community made the purchase, renovation and maintenance of the historic properties possible. The Historical Society conducted a wide variety of fundraisers in the community including antique shows, arts and crafts festivals, masquerade ball, oyster suppers, garden tours, coach tours and street fairs. Many of these events continue to help fund the Society today.

Then, in 1966, when the elegant, eighteenth century Parry Mansion went on the block, the Historical Society gathered their resources, negotiated with Margaret Parry Lang, the fifth generation of the family to have resided there, and saved the historic mansion from becoming a commercial establishment—maybe even a gas station.

In the 1970's the Historical Society completed research to register the houses located in the historic district of New Hope, and was instrumental in creating the borough's Historic and Architectural Review Board that oversees the renovation of historic structures to assure compliance with the standards that have been established to preserve their historic integrity.

In 1990 the Historical Society took the lead and worked with borough government to restore the historic ferry landing.

The historic ferry landing in 2008

The New Hope Historical Society completed extensive renovations to the interior of the barn and replaced the roof in 2007 and 2008. A local landscaper, John Brillman, provided beautiful shrubs for the landscaping of the building. It has never been in greater condition than it is today nearly fifty years after its acquisition by the New Hope Historical Society.

The New Hope Historical Society replaced the roofs of its three eighteenth century structures, and restored deteriorated exterior surfaces of those buildings in 2007. Mindful of its obligation to respect the integrity of these buildings, the Historical Society employed a contractor who used a process first introduced by Paul Revere in 1800. Lead-coated copper strengthens the red cedar shake roofs and looks spectacular. Heating, air conditioning, electrical and security systems have been upgraded—all at a cost of about $200,000. This was possible because of the generosity of its members and supporters and from several grants from the Commonwealth of Pennsylvania.

The Parry Mansion in 2007

Historical societies are as crucially important today as they were in 1958. Just as Dr. Ricker had perceived a groundswell of change that was about to transform communities in the 1950's and 1960's it is clear that our communities are undergoing rapid changes in demographics and economics. It was difficult for the Historical Society's founders to rally financial support to save two of the most beautiful eighteenth century buildings. Today it is nearly impossible. The escalating cost of real estate presents a far greater challenge than our founders had faced. Public, private and non-profit partnerships are the key to preservation today.

A primary responsibility of the Historical Society is to preserve an understanding of the culture of our past for future generations by providing educational opportunities. The New Hope Historical Society maintains the Parry Mansion as a museum to display five periods of art, décor and culture ranging from 1775 to 1900. The décor was inspired by the world-renowned designer of Newport, Rhode Island, Charles Lamar. Docents provide tours of the Parry Mansion throughout the year to continue the understanding of our legacy.

> **Just as Dr. (Arthur J.) Ricker had perceived a groundswell of change that was about to transform communities in the 1950's and 1960's it is clear that our communities are undergoing rapid changes in demographics and economics...and partnerships are the key to (historic) preservation today.**

Walking tours of New Hope offer a presentation of the history and diversity of our local architecture as well as an understanding of our rich heritage from the American Revolution. New Hope History Day involves the whole community in an annual celebration of its rich history. Advanced Placement students from the junior class of New Hope-Solebury High School prepare projects and compose essays that demonstrate the town's history. They are joined by the Coryell's Ferry Militia Re-enactment group, the Greater New Hope Chamber of Commerce, The New Hope Eagle Fire Department and New Hope borough officials and agencies in the annual parade. The Historical Society has installed ten new historic markers at strategic places around the historic district that describe the history of each location. It fascinates visitors and residents alike when they learn about the phases of the community's development from an industrial, mill town to a center of transportation for canal boats, then as a haven for artists in the Pennsylvania Impressionist period and Broadway summer theater to its current standing as the number one tourist attraction in Bucks County and the increase in population that has grown to more than 2,500 residents—more than twice the size of the community that had existed when Dr. Ricker began his quest.

The New Hope Historical Society celebrated its fiftieth anniversary in 2008. Members continue their work to preserve and maintain the two most beautiful and historic structures in town—the Parry Mansion and Parry Barn. Ever aware of Dr. Arthur J. Ricker's dream to preserve New Hope's great history, the Society continues to monitor the condition of the historic district and conducts frequent historic walking tours and educational events each year.

CHAPTER 8

New Places in Old Spaces

More than one hundred buildings in the historic district have been preserved in New Hope. They have been included on the historic register, thanks to the diligent research and long hours of work by Ann Niessen for the New Hope Historical Society in the 1970's. Still, as times have changed, so has the environment and appearance of the town. A number of old landmarks have disappeared through natural or man-made disasters or, in some cases, neglect. Prior to the establishment of the Historic and Architectural Review Board there was little, if any, oversight and control over their preservation. Some structures still remain, but have been transformed for twenty-first century uses. Following are some of the buildings and places in New Hope that have been reintroduced in revised formats to the new generation of residents and visitors.

A Transformed Logan Inn Has Served Guests for Nearly Three Hundred Years

John Wells, considered by most historians to be the founder of New Hope, arrived around 1717. Indeed, the town was named, Wells Ferry, for a generation. He established the ferry where Lenni-Lenape Indians most probably had crossed the Delaware River much earlier, and he obtained the earliest tavern license in the area in 1727. The hotel, now known as the Logan Inn, was originally the Ferry Inn, then Coryell's Tavern and later the Logan House as seen in the photo below.

During the 1940's the Logan Inn was a favorite gathering place for notable entertainers and writers such as Dorothy Parker, George S. Kaufman and S.J. Perelman among many others.

The Logan House in the 1880's

Ironically, the Logan Inn was, in a sense, the birthplace of the New Hope Historical Society. Dr. Arthur Ricker, the first president of the Historical Society, had an office directly across the street from the Logan Inn. He and a small group of local businessman lunched at the Logan Inn almost every day. Their discussions invariably centered on the vast importance of preserving New Hope's art, culture and historic buildings and led to the creation of the New Hope Historical Society in 1958.

The Logan Inn in 2008

The hotel served as a hospital during the Revolutionary War and has undergone numerous renovations and expansion during its nearly three centuries of existence.

Old General Store Continues to Serve as Popular Local Book Shop

For more than two hundred and fifty years the building now occupied by Farley's Book Shop has served Bucks County residents as a commercial store. It is believed to have been one of the earliest general stores in Bucks County. Historian Margaret Bye Richie has noted that the old sign for Parry's General Store was still hanging on the north side of the building in 1940—more than 150 years after New Hope's father, Benjamin Parry, opened his store.

The north side of the building was probably constructed by Benjamin Canby before 1750, more than a generation before Parry arrived in, then, Coryell's Ferry to begin his illustrious career as an entrepreneur. It was originally operated by Beswick and Pryor. .

It is believed that one of the first robberies reported in Bucks County took place at the building when it was still a very small, fledgling general store just about two months from the time that Parry and his brother, Thomas, purchased the store.

Farley's Book Shop in 2008

The south side of the building, long occupied by a unique gift shop named "Strawberry Jam," was added around 1830 when Benjamin Parry was expanding his Parry Barn and Parry Mansion nearby. This occurred around the time when the Delaware Canal was reaching completion in the New Hope area and there was a growing need for food provisions and supplies.

About a hundred years later after Prohibition the store was a tap room with a barber shop in the rear. It became a cooperative grocery store shortly after it was remodeled by noted New Hope architect, Donald Hedges, until closing around 1961. The photo above shows the book shop today where, in the past, fresh fish, tomatoes and asparagus were sold before it became Joseph Welter's antiques shop.

Farley's Book Shop has been an oasis for book lovers for nearly forty years and remains one of New Hope's greatest treasures both architecturally and culturally.

The Bucks County Playhouse—Formerly the Parry Grist Mill

Looking at the Bucks County Playhouse from South Main Street it is difficult to imagine that just seventy five years ago it was a working mill producing hundreds of barrels of flour each week. The mill had originally been constructed in the 1760's, but fire destroyed it in 1790. Benjamin Parry rebuilt the mill about a year later. The south side of the playhouse where audiences are seated once housed the mill operations. The tall structure on the north side of the playhouse was added around 1939 after the playhouse was created.

> **Benjamin Parry was "a man of considerable scientific attainment, having patented one or more useful inventions...who was public spirited, and took interest in all that would improve his neighborhood and county.**

All of the property along the Delaware River from the Ferry Landing Park to the Bucks County Playhouse belonged to Benjamin Parry who is considered by many to be the father of New Hope. Parry also had rights to the river for one mile on each side of the ferry landing. He purchased the mill from Margaret Todd around 1789 and expanded the operations adding more than sixteen acres in the center of New Hope, then Coryell's Ferry, to his property.

Historian, W.W.H. Davis characterizes Benjamin Parry as "a man of considerable scientific attainment, having patented one or more useful inventions… who was public spirited, and took interest in all that would improve his neighborhood or the county."

The Bucks County Playhouse built into the old mill

According to Gilda Morigi, author of *The Difference Began at the Footlights: A Story of Bucks County Playhouse*, the playhouse was conceived in an evening of the summer of 1938 at the home of Susan Palmer, proprietor of a well known New York restaurant. After months of scrambling to raise funds for the construction and after meeting resistance, skepticism form the local townspeople, a flood, a fire and late-arriving seats and stage, the Bucks County Playhouse opened on July 1, 1939—one hundred years after the death of Benjamin Parry, the owner of the mill from which the playhouse was constructed. New Hope resident and community leader, Don Walker, who completed orchestrations for such great Broadway hits as *Oklahoma* and *Fiddler on a Roof*, was a leading figure in the formation of the Playhouse. St. John Terrell and Mike Ellis became the new producers of plays where Parry had produced flour for more than fifty years. Young actors continue to pursue their dreams on the same stage that once introduced some of the greatest names in theater history.

Joshua Ely's House Becomes a Classic French Restaurant, La Bonne Auberge

Thousands of years before Joshua Ely built his magnificent Georgian Style fieldstone farmhouse around 1780 the Lenni-Lenape Indians roamed the one hundred and thirty acre tract and cultivated orchards on the hill. Early Dutch and, later, English settlers followed suit and operated their orchards there. Now, the farm that once housed the Ely family is home to more than one third of New Hope's residents in the Village 2 and Riverwoods developments. Orchards have been replaced by upscale home and condominiums with tennis courts and a state-of-the-art swim club located in a grand park-like setting with an award-winning, fine French restaurant, La Bonne Auberge.

History buffs who reside there delight in the knowledge that the far northern end of the property reached as far away as what is now known as West Mechanic Street. The high ridge that crosses through the former Ely property and the old school was the site of one of three redoubts that had been thrown up by General George Washington's soldiers in 1776 on their march to the Battle of Trenton.

New Hope's father, Benjamin Parry, owned about twelve acres of the Ely property for nearly twenty-five years before selling it back to the Ely's in 1834.

The farm house was built in two sections. The east section is larger and is probably the older part of the house. At close range the difference in the stone work also reveals the difference in age of the two sections.

The Joshua Ely House is now La Bonne Auberge Restaurant

This gorgeous setting with its rolling hills and vista offers a spectacular view of the Delaware River and is crowned by Ely's residence that is really a "Manor" in the true sense of the word, and one of the most elegant still standing in New Hope. In the early 1970's the current owners, Gerard and Rozanne Caronello, renovated and added on to the structure, creating what continues to be one of Bucks County's most charming and top-rated restaurants. They constructed fine redwood decks and beautifully landscaped gardens that lead to the elegant La Bonne Auberge restaurant. Original interior and exterior wood doors, shutters and trim and cupboards, mantel and flooring delight visitors more than two centuries after the Ely family enjoyed them.

The Old Town Hall is now the bustling New Hope Visitors Center

Old Town Hall in 1958

Although it had been called "New Hope" since the early 1790's, New Hope was officially incorporated as a borough in 1837. Two years later it completed construction of its new Town Hall that opened in 1839 on land located at the southwest corner of South Main and West Mechanic Streets. It was purchased for one dollar. It served as the municipal building and jail for nearly a hundred years until the borough moved into its new offices in a converted fire station. The building, located in the center of town across the street from the oldest house in town, was an ideal location for the new visitor center. Today, the original old jail gates from 1839 have been converted into garden trellises that greet thousands of visitors each year at the entrance to the visitor center as the borough prepares for another transformation— moving the borough hall to the former Saint Martin's Catholic Church and rectory, just two blocks west of its original location.

The Oldest Frame House in Town Becomes an Award-Winning Crafts and Jewelry Shop

The location of the house known locally as the Coolbaugh/Flood House on 28 South Main Street could be a great theme for an Abbot and Costello routine. The front of the house on South Main Street is really the back of the house. The back of the house facing the Delaware River is really the front of the house. Confused yet? The house faced the old Riverside Road when it was completed. But the perceived "front" faced River Road, after Riverside Road had been relocated, until it was called Front Street and then, finally, Main Street. Anyway, no matter how one looks at it, this house with its final additions completed around 1801 continues to be one of New Hope's architectural gems. Today it houses a wonderfully unique crafts shop for the home and garden and a fine jewelry shop in the heart of the historic district.

The Coolbaugh-Flood House in 2008

Cornelius Coolbaugh, a local merchant, purchased the land from John Beaumont around 1800 for about $300. The original part of the structure was built around 1764. He completed the additions which are constructed on two separate parcels of land around 1801. Records indicate that by 1839 Beaumont had bought the house back from Coolbaugh and bequeathed it to his son Andrew Jackson. It is the oldest wood frame house in New Hope. The original wood plank floors are stunning.

No one has ever lived in the house longer than New Hope's beloved Dr. John A. Flood. Dr. Flood was a dentist for sixty years and resided in the house for thirty-one years until his death in 1981 when he was ninety-one years old. The little cottage that housed his dental office can still be seen behind what is now the front of the house. His election as mayor of New Hope three times in 1925, 1949 and 1957 attests to his enduring popularity throughout the borough over an extended period of time.

> **"It (New Hope) has always been a lovely place to live, but it took the artists to show me."**

Dr. Flood purchased the home in 1950 and completely restored it. He even furnished the house with authentic antiques portraying its long history. He was a familiar figure to townspeople and tourists alike as he sat on his porch on South Main Street on weekends and enjoyed watching and talking with the wide variety of folks passing by. He was an ardent lover of art and did his utmost to encourage young artists like Redfield, Garber, Lathrop and Leith-Ross, often paying them more for their paintings than their asking price. Some artists even paid their dental bills with their artwork. His tribute to the local artists is eloquent. "It (New Hope) has always been a lovely place to live, but it took the artists to show me," he once said. And what Dr. Flood liked most about New Hope was "the people." And they truly loved him back.

Bed and Breakfast Inn Once an Innovative Grand Home

If your wife asks you to build her the largest house in town, why not throw in running water—the first house with running water in town, and really impress her? That's just what George Cook did. And, to be sure, it was no easy feat. To accomplish his goal, Cook purchased the land directly across the street from what is now the Mansion Inn at 9 South Main Street in 1869. He built and operated a hardware store there that eventually became Cryer's Hardware Store at 20 South Main Street.

The Cook-Leiby Mansion in the early 1900's

Cook connected the hardware store property to the house by two pipe systems. He built a windmill pump behind the hardware store that pumped water from the Delaware River through the pipe across South Main Street and up to a wooden storage tank located on the third floor of the mansion. From there, the force of gravity supplied water to the wash stands on the second floor bedrooms, bathrooms and kitchen. Another pipe was installed to transport rainwater from the roof and across the street to the river.

The Mansion Inn in 2008

To make sure that there were no problems with deliveries to the new mansion, Cook obtained the right of way into the rear of the property from West Bridge Street so that wagons and other vehicles could come and go while having enough space to deliver a load of hay.

Both properties were sold at sheriff's sale in 1900, and after several changes in ownership, the mansion was purchased by Dr. Kenneth Leiby and his wife, Winifred in 1935. They raised their family there and Dr. Leiby established his practice there as well. The beloved physician is known to have collected a variety of fine art from young artists, like Redfield and Garber who paid their medical bills with their paintings long before they became the prominent figures in the art world that they are today. Sixty years later the house, having fallen into considerable disrepair and in danger of conversion to shops after Dr. Leiby's retirement, was purchased and restored to the magnificent structure that now houses an upscale bed and breakfast with a top-rated restaurant.

The Old Union Mills Become Up-Market Condominiums

The original section of the two-story structure is stone and is now the center of the cluster of buildings comprised of brick, stone and steel.

Waterworks Condominiums

In recent years the Union Mills Paper Manufacturing Company buildings located at 350 South Main Street were purchased by the Scannapieco Development Corporation. Today the solid brick and stone structures provide beautiful, upscale condominiums in a uniquely picturesque setting that incorporates deep, historical significance from our nation's Revolutionary War and industrial development periods

Hiram Ely House Once Stood on the Site of Lenape Park

When Elias Ely sold the land at 52 West Ferry Street to Hiram Ely, in 1830 he most probably never dreamed that one hundred and seventy-five years later it would become a public park for the entire town to enjoy.

Hiram Ely, a coach maker, built the three story fieldstone house that graced the northwest corner of West Ferry Street and Stockton Avenue for one and three quarters of a century. The handsome wood cornices and lattice work on the porch adorned the house topped by the sturdy, raised-seem metal roof until the house was devastated by an explosion and fire in March, 2005. Fortunately, those residents who had occupied the house at that time escaped.

The Hiram Ely House

Hiram Ely sold the home to his brother, Brittain Ely, about seventeen years later and then bought it back about seventeen years after that in 1865. Hiram Ely died in 1875.

In 1890 a small section of the land was sold to the North East Pennsylvania Railroad Company which later merged under the Reading Company. The small portion was used by the railroad to build a retaining wall along the railroad tracks when the New Hope station opened in 1891.

The Ely Family was one of the most prominent "dynasties" in New Hope's history. Joshua Ely owned more than one hundred and thirty acres including the land that is now occupied by the Village 2 and Riverwoods complexes. George Ely and his family lived just up the street from Hiram in what is certainly one of the oldest houses in New Hope, now the location of an art gallery at 80 West Ferry Street.

Lenape Park

Lenape Park, opened in 2008, pays tribute to the Lenni-Lenape Indians who first cut the trail leading from Philadelphia to New Hope thousands of years ago and which eventually became Old York Road around 1700. West Ferry Street is the final portion of that road in Pennsylvania ending at the Ferry Landing Park. The road continued in Lambertville, New Jersey winding its way north to New York City.

An Original Old School House Makes a Comfortable Home Today

Thousands of vehicles including jammed school buses ride by the house on 129 West Bridge Street regularly. But the unassuming, sand plaster over fieldstone structure discreetly hides the story of its great role in the history of New Hope's educational system. It was one of the original schools in New Hope and most probably the first public school for girls.

Later known as "The Academy," the home was built around 1843 by William Umpleby. He was the owner of the Lepanto Mills, currently known as the Old Mill Apartments located on Old Mill Road in New Hope. The mills were located just about a block from Umpleby's home. At that time Umpleby resided just two houses east of the structure. His home is now a fashionable Bed and Breakfast Inn.

The Academy in 2008

The Academy served as a public school for young ladies until around 1851 when the "new" school on the hill above West Mechanic Street was completed. It had also been used for Sunday school sessions for a few years. The "new" school is now home to the Kehilat Ha Nahar, a Reconstructionist synagogue. This is the grand structure that had been immortalized by Joseph Pickett in his painting entitled, Manchester Valley, that now hangs in the Museum of Modern Art in New York City.

There is another note of distinction for the old Academy building. It was the birthplace and boyhood home of Jake Fell, the beloved councilman, now retired, who served the Borough of New Hope for thirty-five years and presided at his last council session as President in December, 2005.

The Academy building has been altered numerous times and had been a private residence for more than a hundred and thirty years. More recently it was used for a shop, but it is once again a private dwelling.

Old High School Served a Variety of Purposes is now a Synagogue

The Museum of Modern Art in New York City houses Joseph Pickett's most famous work, "Manchester Valley." Dominating the painting is an oversized depiction of the old school house atop the hill over West Mechanic Street. Pickett was a canal boat builder and worked at a variety of tasks including carpentry, shooting gallery operator and grocer. He turned to painting at the age of nearly sixty five years. Pickett donated the painting to the New Hope school where it was displayed until 1939.

The Old School around 1870

Although the school house may be oversized in the painting, perhaps, in retrospect, it is a statement of the structure's wide variety of uses over more than one hundred and fifty years. The building was purchased by the New Hope Borough School Directors in 1850. It continued to be a school for the primary grades until 1938. Upper grades attended classes in mail-order-type buildings that resembled barracks, purchased from Sears, Roebuck and Company, that were located outside the main building. These smaller buildings were gradually sold by the borough of New Hope. The students in the upper grades were moved to the New Hope High School when it opened in 1931 at 180 West Bridge Street. The school district sold the old property in 1941 and the ownership changed hands a couple of times. It was used for a stained glass studio by Valentine d'Ogries and then passed to Dr. Kenneth Leiby until it was purchased by Albert's Old School House Inn, Inc. in 1961.

Albert Conrad Huber ran his Old School House Inn for several years, and New Hope has probably never seen anything like it before or since that time. He was widely known as New Hope's "Renaissance Man" who loved young ladies and, at times, resembled Picasso with his waxed mustache and Liberace with his sequined sneakers. The New Hope Gazette reported that Albert once refused to seat a party for dinner, because they had no reservations, even tough his restaurant was empty at the time. And it is said that he once ordered a customer to leave the restaurant for requesting ketchup for Albert's specialty potatoes. Despite his eccentricities it was reported that the Swiss-born man of many talents, a tool maker, writer and musician. He was very much loved by those who knew him.

New Hope's popular restaurateur and community icon, Pamela Minford, owned the school house property for about thirty years until selling it to the Kehilat HaNahar, a Jewish Reconstructionist synagogue in 1996. The Little Shul, as it is known now provides a gathering place for worship, education and community activities for New Hope's Jewish population in a forest-like setting atop the hill where George Washington's troops once defended the town from the British troops by establishing a redoubt nearby during the Revolutionary War.

The Old Methodist Church is now a Top-Rated Restaurant

For one hundred and twenty-five years the United Methodist Church provided spiritual guidance and education to thousands of its congregation at its location at 15 South Main Street. It was the second building constructed by the church which experienced continued growth since beginning in a private home in Lambertville, New Jersey around 1830 About seven years later the congregation dedicated a modest building at the southwest corner of West Mechanic and New Streets in New Hope. The old cemetery is located along the driveway to the former Saint Martin's Roman Catholic Church which is currently being transformed into the new borough hall and police headquarters for New Hope.

The Old Methodist Church around 1880

But growth continued and soon the congregation was looking for more space in a more central location. So, around 1865 they began exploring a better site for their growing number of members. Reverend Joseph F. DiPaolo, a former pastor of the United Methodist Church in New Hope credits Reverend Lucian B. Brown for his determination and energy that led to the purchase of land on South Main Street, then River Road, and getting the new church built. The "Panic of 1873" devastated financial markets leading to the postponement of the construction. Although Reverend Brown had moved on, the church that he so strongly advocated was finally dedicated in 1880. Reverend DiPaolo, in his publication *The Story of a Church Home* recalls the words of Pastor Amos Johnson at the dedication of the church: "... we have a beautiful temple for the worship of God and I hope that hope that he will glorify himself in this house of glory." The fervor and generosity of the congregation made it possible for the church to pay the debts for construction completely by 1888.

Marsha Brown's Restaurant in 2008

Population changes and the inability of the United Methodist Church to expand its facility on South Main Street led the congregation, once again, to plan another church to serve its needs. So, in 1998, the church that was valued at $14,000 when it was completed in 1880 was sold for $750,000, and just about two years later the congregation moved into its beautiful new campus on Aquetong Road in nearby Solebury Township, Pennsylvania.

It is somewhat surreal to enter the old church building today. Widely popular for her restaurant savvy and for the charm and southern hospitality that she exudes, Marsha Brown has transformed the church into a dazzling destination for those seeking nourishment for their bodies. The choir loft is now a handsomely appointed meeting area with a gleaming cocktail bar. The sanctuary, where hymnals once were the publications of choice, is now festooned with neat dinner tables bearing fancily printed, refined, Creole menus for the hungry diners' perusal. And Marsha Brown seems to wax religious when she describes her restaurant as "…an environment where souls are moved into peace and comfort through selected textures, quiet colors and engaging hospitality."

Stately Victorian Home of Joseph E. Reeder Now Houses Guests as an Inn

Just when it appears that the entire great array of architectural treasures in town has been exhausted and visitors are exiting New Hope via West Bridge Street a pleasant surprise awaits them just before the modern shopping center at the western edge of town. The Joseph E. Reeder House, in all its Victorian splendor, waves an elegant good-bye to all who pass its gorgeous wooden doors and gabled dormer gracefully placed in a mansard roof. It also welcomes visitors in its recent role as a charming bed and breakfast inn.

The Joseph Reeder House

Records indicate that Joseph Reeder owned the house around 1876 and lived there until his death in 1893. Later, it was in the McDonnell family for more than six decades. It has been suggested that the house could have been built around the early 1830's by William Maris, who had built his Portuguese-inspired mansion across the Old York Road from the Reeder home. Some of the construction materials for both houses are similar, but the architecture is completely different; the former looking rather palatial while the latter represents a Victorian style farm house.

The home has been enlarged a number of times. First, on the north side, the back of the house was added most probably to accommodate a growing family. Later, a section was added to the western side to provide expanded space for the Bed and Breakfast Inn that now serves travelers more than one hundred and seventy-five years after it was built.

Eastburn Reeder, the son of Joseph Reeder was one of the most prominent gentlemen of Bucks County in his time. He had one of the finest herds of Jersey cattle in Bucks County. He was manager of the Lahaska-New Hope Turnpike Company. He served on the Solebury School board for nine years; and in 1893 he was appointed the first State Dairy and Food Commissioner after serving for sixteen years as the Bucks County representative to the State Board of Agriculture. He had been married to Ellen Kenderdine. The Reeder-Eastburn-Kenderdine families represent three of the oldest and most prominent families in Bucks County history.

Union Camp Bag Company Is Now Union Square

On the south end of town the Union Paper Mill manufactured bag paper which was sold to companies that made paper bags. A shrewd management decision to build a manufacturing plant in New Hope that made bags maximized the company's profits. When the Union Paper Mill switched to manufacturing insulating paper for electrical connections, the bag mill had been making bags for ice and charcoal. The business was not doing well at the old Race Street location, now, Old Mill Road, and management was about to move the operations to Lambertville, New Jersey. The railroad's decision to construct a building next to the train station for the operations in New Hope saved the plant for the town. In 1979 the New Hope Gazette reported that the Union Camp Bag Company was the town's largest employer with a work force of 115 employees and annual wages totaling one million dollars. The planned expansion at that time promised about 25 new jobs. They manufactured heavy-duty bags for dog food, livestock feed, cement and chemicals. When the plant closed in 1990 it marked the end of the industrial-manufacturing era in New Hope. The plant was used for various warehouse and storage facilities for several years as it continued to deteriorate into a blighted brown site.

Union Square in 2008

The Union Camp complex was purchased by local developer, George E. Michael and Company, Inc. and, after several years of planning and design, a new, invigorating professional office and shopping complex emerged in 2002 as Union Square. Now, hundreds of professional employees work in the wide range of businesses that have located there including pharmaceutical, telecommunications, investment planning, real estate and research companies. Trendy shops, popular restaurants, a health club and spa make Union Square a popular destination for local residents and visitors.

Union Camp's transformation from a blue collar manufacturing company into a dynamic hub of professional offices, shops, restaurants and art galleries dramatically symbolizes the change that has occurred in the New Hope community over the past century. It gives testimony to the ever-evolving magic of New Hope.

Former Fishery Site a Popular Restaurant

It is a lot easier to get great seafood at this location today than it was two hundred and fifty years ago. All one has to do is sit down and order it! The Landing Restaurant, known far and wide for its fine food is situated on the site that was once a home to New Hope's fishing industry. The lawn of the restaurant was the location of the old fishery site stretching around the back of the building and north to what is now Randolph Street Park. The restaurant was the old Hiram Scarborough home. Scarborough was the last to exercise the rights to shad fishing in New Hope. Faced with continued meager runs of shad, the Scarborough family quit the business in 1942. James Skillman purchased the fishing rights, but never exercised them.

Originally, this area was part of the great Paxson Family's six hundred and twenty-four acres that spread across more than half of New Hope from Sugan Road west to the Delaware River. Joseph Pike and his family, who eventually sold this land to the Paxsons, was the first to operate a shad fishery in New Hope having obtained a fishing patent from William Penn.

During Joseph Pike's time, the Delaware River was most probably the largest shad location along the Atlantic coast. It was well known for its great flavor. John Richardson records that the river fisheries peaked at nineteen million pounds around 1896, but had dwindled to a mere 76,000 pounds by 1954. During the peak years, Isaac Scarborough and his sons owned the fishing rights from the New Hope-Lambertville Bridge north to the Rabbit Run Bridge. William Lewis operated a fishery off Malta Island, and on what was known as "Smoke House" south of Scarborough's site. Lewis Island on the Delaware River is named for him. Shad were packed in ice and shipped to Philadelphia and New York City markets.

The New Jersey side of the river was far better adapted for the fishing industry, but there were also fishing sites in Brownsburg and Point Pleasant in Pennsylvania. In 1899 there were about 400,000 shad caught in a single season. Even as late as 1938 it is said that one thousand shad were caught across the Delaware River in just two days. But a lethal combination of pollution, power boating, construction and low river tables ended the fishing industry in the New Hope area. Only a small remnant of the shad fishery industry survives on the New Jersey side of the river.

Fabled Hacienda Inn Replaced by Upscale Town Homes

In the middle of the nineteenth century the little block at the top of the hill on West Mechanic Street in New Hope was home to mill workers and canal boat tenders. Their homes nestled high above the Aquetong Creek below and just a few hundred feet from the bustling Delaware Canal that, at its peak, carried three thousand canal boats to markets each year. It was a mill town then. Mechanics and canal workers lived there close to the hard work that provided their livelihood.

As the mill industry waned and the last canal boat floated out of town in the 1930's New Hope was becoming known for its attraction to artists. Its natural beauty became a magnet for some of the great Pennsylvania Impressionist painters like Edward Redfield, William Lathrop, Daniel Garber, John Sharp and so many others that followed.

Shortly after the arrival of the artists New Hope's proximity to New York City and Broadway made it an ideal location for summer stock and try-outs for new Broadway shows. By the 1950's the Bucks County Playhouse became the summer stage for Hammerstein, Kaufmann, Hart, Hayes, Redford, George C. Scott and many more.

Pam Minford's Hacienda Inn

Pamela Minford arrived on the New Hope scene just as the popularity and glamour of the town's theater began to spread. And New Hope would never be the same again. Pam loved to entertain. She sold her antiques business which she had originally started in New York at the age of seventeen and had brought to New Hope in the early 1950's. Beginning with a cozy and instantly popular El Patio, Pam enlarged the space and added a Castilian dining room. Then, for the added convenience of her beloved guests, she built thirty-four rooms for lodging and added dining rooms, a cocktail lounge, a swimming pool and a parking lot. New Hope residents were soon rubbing elbows with Maurice Chevalier, Robert Goulet, Bert Reynolds, Dinah Shore, Ella Fitzgerald, Wayne Newton, Victor Borge, Liberace, Kaye Ballard, Sandy Dennis and so many others as they dined at Pam's Hacienda. And Pam treated everyone who came to her Hacienda as stars. Her business ventures grew at such a varied and fast pace that she was once called "the Howard Hughes of New Hope" by a Philadelphia newspaper.

> **No doubt Broadway and Hollywood stars and just plain, ordinary people still come to town looking for Pam's great get-away.**

New Hope lost Pam Minford several years ago, but her kindness, generosity, love for entertaining guests and her entrepreneurship will long be remembered by Broadway and Hollywood stars and local folks alike. The Hacienda Inn continued as a restaurant and inn for a brief period after Pam had sold it to concentrate her efforts on her Fabulous Fountainhead conference center that she created less than a mile from her original success.

Canal Street

Today, there is little trace of the old Hacienda Inn on West Mechanic Street. The oldest section of the inn that was built in the mid-1800's was preserved as an integral part of the new Canal Street Town Homes. Mill and canal workers would certainly marvel to see the distinctive four-level homes with private interior elevators, spacious outdoor decks, two-car, attached garages and a beautiful new park in place of their old humble abodes. And, no doubt, Broadway and Hollywood stars and just plain, ordinary people still come to town looking for Pam's great get-away. The new residents of Canal Street occupy one of the most fascinating sites in New Hope's long and colorful history.

The Quaker Spirit of Hope and Determination Continues in New Hope

Over the past three hundred years New Hope's serenity and natural beauty have been jolted many times. The town has been devastated by floods in each of the centuries. A massive fire in the early twentieth century destroyed a section in the north end of the borough. A fire and gas explosion in the early part of this century destroyed one of New

Hope's oldest homes, the Hiram Ely House. After each of the disasters New Hope has always come back. The tragic floods that ravaged New Hope in the past one hundred years failed to destroy the community's enthusiasm and vigor.

The early nineteenth century home that was destroyed by fire just a few years ago has been replaced with a beautiful new neighborhood park named in honor of the Lenni-Lenape Native Americans. In the true spirit of the Native Americans' love of the land, New Hope has created five pocket parks providing relaxing, green spaces around town.

In the Quaker tradition of hope Benjamin Parry rebuilt his mills that had been devastated by fire more than two centuries ago. That same spirit led local businessman and resident, Michael Amery, to begin the reconstruction of the eighteenth century Odette's River House restaurant that once housed mill workers and canal builders. The widely popular inn was ravaged again by flooding in 2006 after two previous floods within two years. Plans call for the old Odette's River House to be resurrected in a new, expanded setting that will highlight the grand, late eighteenth century structure.

New Hope Visitor Center Today

As the twenty-first century unfolded New Hope's revitalization continued. It remains the number one tourist destination in Bucks County, Pennsylvania and attracts visitors from all parts of the United States. Its population, at 2,500 residents, is the largest in its history. The borough government's proposal for an innovative plan for the enhancement of the Delaware River waterfront would vastly expand access to the river and create new opportunities for recreation, shopping and entertainment in the heart of the historic district where the late Dr. Arthur J. Ricker began his work in 1958. Dr Ricker would most probably be very pleased to know that nearly half of the Borough of New Hope Community Revitalization Committee members are also directors of the New Hope Historical Society, and that his legacy and commitment endure.

CPSIA information can be obtained at www.ICGtesting.com
Printed in the USA
BVOW050410201011

274093BV00005B/1/P